Student's Manual to Accompany

The United States Since 1865

by Foster Rhea Dulles

Student's Manual to Accompany THE UNITED STATES SINCE 1865 BY FOSTER RHEA DULLES

Prepared by Warren A. Beck

Ann Arbor

The University of Michigan Press

Published in the United States of America by
The University of Michigan Press and simultaneously
in Toronto, Canada, by Ambassador Books Limited
Manufactured in the United States of America

Paperback ISBN: 978-0-472-75116-7

Foreword

To the question, how does one study history, there is no single answer. The techniques used will vary widely. What will be successful for one student will not work for another. A study pattern evolved for one instructor may have to be altered for another. However, there is an approach to the study of history that has proved universally successful. A mastery of the material covered in the textbook is still a basic approach to the study of history.

To use the *Student's Manual to Accompany The United States Since 1865, by Foster Rhea Dulles* most advantageously it is recommended that the student proceed in the following manner:

1) Study the chapter summaries in the *Manual* in order to obtain an introduction to the material covered.
2) Read the chapter with care seeking to understand and retain the essential material. Either underline the key passages in the text or take notes as necessary.
3) Put the text aside and answer the multiple choice questions in your *Manual*. When completed, check your answers. If you have understood what you have read you should be able to answer most of the questions correctly.
4) Check the terms, events, and personalities to know. Write out the answers to these if necessary.
5) Make an outline answering the essay questions. Some students will want to write their answers to these questions in essay form.
6) In preparing for tests the student should incorporate the material from his class notes with that of the text.
7) The map exercises will make the textual material more meaningful. To complete these exercises consult the maps in your text or a standard historical atlas.

WARREN A. BECK

Contents

CHAPTER I

The Aftermath of War

Summary:

The end of the Civil War settled many basic issues in America. For once and all the question of the supremacy of the national government was resolved. Never again were the states to challenge effectively the authority of Washington. The war brought tremendous economic changes to the North. The development of the factory system to meet the war needs accelerated the transition from an agrarian to an urban economy. The South suffered complete economic ruin. The old order of plantation life resting on slave labor was totally destroyed. What the South needed in the immediate postwar period was economic help, but the issue was treated as a political problem.

Had President Lincoln lived, the transition of the South to a new order might have been easier. The Civil War President had developed reconstruction plans that stressed forgiving the South for its past misdeeds and returning it to an effective place within the political life of the nation as soon as possible. His great prestige and political leadership might have been able to check the vendetta plans of the Radical Republicans led by Charles Sumner and Thaddeus Stevens. President Johnson had neither the prestige nor the leadership ability to accomplish these goals, though he did try to carry out Lincoln's plan of reconstruction. Unfortunately, Southerners played into the hands of the Radical Republicans by seeking to keep the South as it was before the Civil War.

Multiple Choice Questions:

______ **1. In his reconstruction plans President Lincoln desired to 1) appease Congress 2) punish the South 3) return the South to an effective position as soon as possible 4) ensure that the South would vote Republican.**

______ **2. The Wade-Davis Bill 1) embodied Lincoln's reconstruction plan 2) would recognize the seceded states as soon as 10 per cent of the citizens took an oath of allegiance 3) was pleasing to most Southerners 4) embodied the ideas of Congress on Reconstruction.**

_______ 3. President Johnson's reconstruction plans were influenced by 1) his loyalty to the Republican party 2) his desire to extend the powers of the federal government 3) his antipathy for the wealthy Southern planters 4) his defense of the wealthy Southern aristocrats.

_______ 4. Accounting for much of President Johnson's difficulty as President was 1) his aristocratic bearing and manners 2) his numerous appearances while intoxicated 3) his desire to repudiate Lincoln's reconstruction plans 4) his lack of dignity and unwillingness to compromise.

_______ 5. The position of the Radical Republicans who wanted to punish the South for having started the Civil War was strengthened by 1) the passage of the Black Codes 2) President Johnson 3) the decisions of the Supreme Court 4) the passage of the Thirteenth Amendment.

_______ 6. The most important motive of the Radical Republicans in their reconstruction plans was to 1) destroy the ability of the South ever to fight again 2) help the Negro adjust to a free society 3) destroy the power of the President 4) establish the national supremacy of the Republican party.

_______ 7. The Black Codes were passed to 1) force the Negroes to work 2) destroy the political power of the Negroes 3) restore the Negro to the status of chattel slavery 4) counteract the effects of the Fifteenth Amendment.

_______ 8. Most justifiable of the aims of the Radical reconstructionists was their 1) attempt to make political capital out of the situation in the South 2) attempt to punish the South for having seceded 3) attempt to obtain equality for the Negro in the South 4) denial of citizenship to former Confederates.

_______ 9. The South played into the hands of the Radicals by 1) voting Democrat 2) supporting the scalawags 3) opposing the Fourteenth Amendment 4) refusing to repudiate Confederate debts.

Essay Questions:

1. What made conditions severe in the South after the war? Why was it to be very difficult to revive the prostrate South?

2. What were the essential features of Lincoln's reconstruction plan? Upon what basis did Congress oppose the postwar policy of the Great Emancipator?

3. How did Johnson's reconstruction plans differ from those of Lincoln? In what ways were they similar? Why did Johnson have so much difficulty in carrying out his program?

4. Compare and contrast the reconstruction plans of Sumner and Stevens. Why was the North more ready to accept their views than those of Johnson?

5. How did the South play into the hands of the Radicals and help seal the fate of the region during Reconstruction?

6. If Lincoln had lived, would his approach to Reconstruction have encountered the same difficulties that the program of President Johnson did? Or was the victory of the Radicals virtually predestined? Argue this point.

Terms, Events, and Personalities to Know:

Wade-Davis Bill
"drunken tailor"
Freedmen's Bureau
Civil Rights Bill
"Black Codes"
Fourteenth Amendment
Radicals

CHAPTER II

Reconstruction and Recovery

Summary:

In the congressional elections of 1866 the Radical Republicans obtained a two-thirds majority in both houses of Congress. This made it possible for them to override presidential measures, thus freeing them from whatever restraints had existed before. They destroyed the Lincoln-Johnson concept of Reconstruction and replaced it with their own version of how the South should be treated. When President Johnson attempted to stand in their way he was impeached for "high crimes and misdemeanors." Fortunately, the charges failed to be upheld by a single vote. However, Congress was able to construct its own kind of government in the South. The state governments created under the presidential plan were removed, and the South was divided into five military districts administered by the Army. Puppet state governments were established in the military districts with Negroes, carpetbaggers, and scalawags in control. Frequently, these governments were manipulated by outsiders and were marked by outlandish graft and corruption.

The white Southerners did not accept their position of inferiority willingly. They resisted whenever possible. Actually, the Congressional governments were kept in office only by the power of Northern bayonets. The newly enfranchised Negroes were intimidated by means of such organizations as the Ku Klux Klan, and once the federal troops were removed from the South the whites were soon in control again. The Negroes' position in the system of sharecropping was only a little superior to what it had been before the Civil War. Once political reconstruction ended, the economic reconstruction of the South began. By the end of the nineteenth century a new South had emerged, with considerable emphasis on manufacturing and on the exploitation of natural resources in place of the old emphasis on agriculture and cotton.

Multiple Choice Questions:

_____ **1. Johnson provided the Radicals with the excuse they were seeking for impeachment when he challenged the 1) Thirteenth Amendment 2) creation of the Freedmen's Bureau 3) Fourteenth Amendment 4) Tenure of Office Act.**

_____ **2. If Johnson had been removed as President 1) The South would have been punished for having started the Civil War 2) the powers of the executive branch of the government would have been dangerously impaired 3) the powers of Congress would have been lessened 4) the Democratic party would have been virtually destroyed.**

_____ **3. The main difference between "carpetbaggers" and "scalawags" was that the 1) latter were from the North 2) carpetbaggers were supporters of the Radicals 3) scalawags were Southerners who supported Congressional reconstruction 4) carpetbaggers were Southerners who supported Congressional reconstruction.**

_____ **4. The purpose of the Fifteenth Amendment was to 1) grant the Negro the vote 2) free the Negro from bondage 3) make the Negroes citizens 4) enable Congress to remove President Johnson from office.**

_____ **5. The reconstruction governments established in the Southern states 1) had the popular support of most of the whites in those states 2) failed to obtain the backing of the newly enfranchised Negro 3) remained in power only with the backing of Northern bayonets 4) were models of efficiency.**

_____ **6. Reconstruction in the South officially ended in 1) 1868 2) 1877 3) 1872 4) 1880.**

_____ **7. The last Southern states to be freed of radical Reconstruction were 1) Texas, Tennessee, Arkansas 2) Florida, Virginia, North Carolina 3) Alabama, Mississippi, Georgia 4) Louisiana, South Carolina, Florida.**

_____ **8. The long-range effect of Congressional Reconstruction of the South 1) ruined the South economically 2) led to many lasting reforms 3) created the Solid South politically 4) broke the power of the Democratic party in the South.**

_____ **9. Southern state governments during Reconstruction 1) enacted several needed reform measures 2) accomplished nothing constructive 3) were so well operated that governmental costs were kept to a minimum 4) would permit no Southerners to participate.**

_____ **10. The rapid recovery of Southern agriculture in the postwar period was characterized by 1) wholesome diversification 2) the importation of many Europeans as laborers 3) undue emphasis upon the production of cotton 4) failure to get the Negro to work in the fields.**

Essay Questions:

1. What were the basic issues involved in the impeachment of President Johnson? What would have happened to the powers of the presidency had he been convicted?

2. Describe the general character of government under Reconstruction in the South. What were some of the good features of these governments?

3. Why was the failure of the governments established under Reconstruction inevitable? Discuss the techniques used by the Southern aristocrats to regain political control.

4. What has been the long-range political effect of the Reconstruction Era?

5. What was the nature of the economy in the New South that emerged after Reconstruction?

Terms, Events, and Personalities to Know:

Solid South	**Force Act**
Fifteenth Amendment	**Ku Klux Klan**
Tenure of Office Act	**"redeemers"**
"scalawags"	**"carpetbaggers"**

CHAPTER III

The Last Frontier: Gold, Cattle, and Wheat

Summary:

Throughout the early history of the United States the frontier acted as a safety valve whenever conditions were not good in the rest of the country. Restless people could always move to the frontier, where land was easy to obtain. Between 1865 and 1890 the last frontier in American history was settled. Gold and silver provided the initial magnet which attracted the settlers. The railroads made possible rapid movement into the wide expanse of the Great Plains. Before the settlements could be placed on a permanent basis in the vast area west of the Mississippi the Indians had to be removed. The federal government was to accomplish this by using the military. Once the Indians were gone in the West herdsmen began an era of grazing which assumed greater proportions than ever before. The open-range system was profitable for more than a decade. These years have immortalized the cowboy of legend. Following the herdsman were the farmers, who moved into the Plains country assuming that it would be as easy to adjust to this area as it had been to adjust to the Midwest. The invention of barbed wire and the use of the windmill made the transition to this land possible. Farming conditions, however, were vastly different from those in the Midwest or in the East. Long distances to market, periodic drouth, and grasshopper plagues made farming on the Great Plains a most hazardous venture.

Multiple Choice Questions:

______ **1. Which of the following failed to live up to its early promise as a gold mining state? 1) California 2) South Dakota 3) Idaho 4) Colorado.**

______ **2. A significant by-product of the mining frontier was that 1) the lure of immediate riches helped open the West to permanent settlement 2) it brought the cattle industry to the mountain area 3) it led to the development of a transcontinental railroad 4) it led to better understanding with the Plains Indians.**

______ **3. The "Great American Desert" roughly includes the area bounded by 1) Missouri and Colorado 2) the Mississippi and the Pacific coast 3) the 94th meridian and the Rockies 4) the 100th meridian and the Rio Grande.**

______ **4. Which of the following was NOT true of the building of the transcontinental railroads? 1) Great engineering skill was displayed. 2) Generous government subsidies were granted. 3) The cost of these railroads to the American people was less than their actual cost. 4) Fraud and corruption were common.**

______ **5. The main cause of the conflict that led to Custer's defeat was 1) the attempt of Sitting Bull to organize the Plains Indians into a giant confederation 2) the extermination of an Indian group by the Army at Sand Creek. 3) the desires of the Apaches to drive out all whites 4) the discovery of gold in the Black Hills.**

______ **6. The role of the cowboy in the development of the West 1) had little or no significance 2) was ended with the Long Drive 3) has been greatly exaggerated 4) has been usually ignored by students of the West.**

______ 7. The basic attraction to the farmer who came west was 1) the great forest areas 2) cheap land 3) a ready market for his produce 4) government assistance.

______ 8. NOT one of the problems of the Plains farmer was 1) the grasshopper plagues 2) the lack of water 3) cold winters and hot summers 4) the lack of fertile soil.

______ 9. The "boomers" were associated with the settlement of 1) the Dakotas 2) Oklahome 3) California 4) Montana.

Essay Questions:

1. Why was the vast area between the 94th meridian and the Rockies considered the Great American Desert? Account for its ultimate settlement.

2. What was the significance of the disappearance of the frontier near the end of the nineteenth century?

3. How did the mining frontier act as a necessary intermediate phase in the settling of the West?

4. To what extent were the railroads indispensable to the building of the West? Was the assistance granted to the railroads by the federal and state governments justified in the long run? Could the railroads have been built with greater efficiency?

5. What made the clash between the Plains Indians and the whites virtually inevitable? How were the Indians finally defeated? Could the Indian problem have been handled differently than it was?

6. Why has the story of the early cattle industry continued to fascinate America?

7. How were the homesteaders able to take over the Plains area from the cattlemen? Should this area have been converted into farms?

Terms, Events, and Personalities to Know:

Joseph F. Glidden
"boomers"
Abilene
Homestead Act
Omnibus Bill
Great American Desert
Frederick Jackson Turner
Joseph G. McCoy
Cripple Creek
Virginia City
Black Hills
Crédit Mobilier
Comstock Lode
Dawes Act
Chisholm Trail

CHAPTER IV

The Growth of Industry

Summary:

Within a few years after the Civil War the United States had developed from a primarily agrarian society to an urban-industrial one. This rapid transition was a direct result of the Civil War, which had stimulated American industry. The United States had all of the factors necessary for the creation of an industrial society: adequate raw material, technology, labor, transportation, and mass markets. To these were added men of vision and imagination who were prepared to create great industries.

The railroads were the first and perhaps the most natural of the great industrial combinations that emerged. Men like Daniel Drew made millions at the expense of the American people, and they bought up legislatures and judges whenever it was necessary. In spite of the abuses which existed, a network of railroads soon spanned the nation and made possible the growth of industry.

The railroads were not the only great monopoly to arise. John D. Rockefeller came to dominate the oil business and Andrew Carnegie the steel industry. J. P. Morgan is best known for his monopoly of the banking business and his development of finance capitalism.

This rapid development of gigantic business enterprises, usually exercising monopolies in their fields, necessitated a theory to justify it. As a result, laissez faire as an economic doctrine was developed, according to which the government had no right to interfere with free enterprise. A claim, based on Darwinian theories of evolution, was made that those who were able to move to the top benefited all of society. The inequities that crept into the Industrial Revolution in America prompted many complaints, especially from the farmers and from labor. However, governmental attempts at regulation through the I.C.C. and the Sherman Act were unsuccessful.

Multiple Choice Questions:

_____ 1. Rockefeller's monopoly of the oil industry enabled him to do all *but* one of the following: 1) introduce economies in the refining of oil 2) make immense profits for Standard Oil 3) grant lower prices to the consumer 4) bring order to the oil industry.

_____ 2. The success of Standard Oil was made possible by all of the following *except* 1) secret rebates from the railroads 2) improved marketing techniques 3) choking off other companies' crude oil supplies 4) Rockefeller's technical innovations in refining.

_____ 3. The Great Northern was unique among Western railroads in that 1) it was the first transcontinental road 2) it received extravagant federal subsidies 3) its profits resulted from a mining boom 4) it received little or nothing in the way of federal subsidies.

_____ 4. In his drive to the top of the business world Andrew Carnegie was NOT aided by 1) an uncanny ability to select competent business associates 2) tremendous personal industry 3) the advantage of fine family connections 4) a flair for promotion and salesmanship.

_____ 5. In general, the entrepreneurs of the post-Civil War era were NOT distinguished by 1) solicitude for the rights of labor 2) drive and imagination 3) greed 4) a willingness to take chances.

_____ 6. Most of the power of the Sherman Anti-Trust Act was removed when the Supreme Court ruled in favor of a monopoly in 1) railroads 2) steel 3) tobacco 4) sugar.

_____ 7. The Interstate Commerce Commission had the power to 1) protest unreasonable rates 2) establish reasonable rates 3) force the railroads to obey its decisions 4) override court decisions.

_____ 8. In attacking the efforts of Granger legislatures to regulate the railroads the main argument used was that these laws 1) were an unfair use of the taxing power 2) violated the Fifth Amendment 3) violated the Fourteenth Amendment 4) were unconstitutional, as the federal government had to regulate commerce.

_____ 9. The constitutionality of the Granger laws to regulate the railroads was first upheld by the Supreme Court in 1) the Minnesota Rate Case 2) *Munn* v *Illinois* 3) the Wabash Case 4) *E. C. Knight Company* v *the United States.*

_____ 10. The best explanation of the popularity of the Gospel of Wealth was 1) it had Biblical sanction 2) it was widely publicized 3) it benefited all of the nation in the long run 4) it benefited a powerful minority.

Essay Questions:

1. Why did the United States experience such a phenomenal growth of industry in the period immediately following the Civil War?

2. Account for the low moral standards of businessmen in the Gilded Age.

3. Compare and contrast the railroad-building activities of Fisk and Gould with those employed by James J. Hill.

4. To what extent was the work of great captains of industry like Carnegie and Rockefeller necessary to the expansion of American business? Would the business community have been better off in the long run without their activities?

5. What was the long-range effect of the rapid growth of monopoly in the business world? Could the trend toward the consolidation of industry have been checked by a more aggressive government policy?

6. How did the advent of finance capitalism bring a greater degree of stability to the business world? Describe Morgan's capabilities.

7. What were the basic economic philosophies of the era? Why was the Gospel of Wealth so attractive to the business community?

8. Describe the attempts by the government to regulate business before 1900. Why were these attempts relatively unsuccessful?

Terms, Events, and Personalities to Know:

ICC
Sherman Act
Gospel of Greed
Great Northern
Munn **v** *Illinois*
Granger movement
Richard Olney
E. C. Knight **v** *the United States*
laissez faire
Gilded Age
Daniel Drew

CHAPTER V

Agriculture and Labor

Summary:

As industry expanded the relative importance of the American farmer tended to decline. The farmer was caught in a changing society which he did not understand. Improved transportation made possible the exploitation of farmlands throughout the United States, but also placed the American farmer in direct competition with other parts of the world which also were experiencing a similar transportation revolution. Improved technology increased yields, thereby depressing prices, while the overhead of the farmer became higher as a result of the necessity to purchase more equipment. The interest rates charged by the bankers were exorbitant because of the risk involved. In the Great Plains the vicissitudes of the weather made farming more hazardous than in other parts of the country. Caught in a declining price and rising cost squeeze, the American farmer saw as his only way out a depression of money values. He supported proposals to print greenbacks and, later, to coin silver, as ways to pay his debts.

Laborers also were faced with problems as a result of the growth of industry. Efforts to organize unions before the Civil War failed for various reasons. The short-lived National Labor Union, the first effective national labor organization, was founded in the first year after the Civil War by William H. Sylvis. It was followed by the Knights of Labor, composed of both skilled and unskilled workers. This group demanded a variety of reforms, governmental and otherwise. It grew rapidly under the leadership of Terence Powderly, but declined after 1886. The American Federation of Labor inherited much of the membership of the Knights. Originally organized in 1881, the A. F. of L. stressed a conservative, nonpolitical policy favorable to private enterprise. Workers in the decades after the Civil War called a number of strikes in order to better their working conditions, but all of them were failures. The disastrous Harvester-McCormick Works strike of 1886 was climaxed by the Haymarket affair. The Homestead strike in 1892 and the Pullman strike two years later resulted in failures for the union. The development of labor unions was hampered because the government invariably favored the position of industry and permitted the use of the injunction, making it virtually impossible for labor to use the strike effectively.

Multiple Choice Questions:

______ **1. The best explanation of American farmers' interest in cheap money was that they 1) were usually in debt 2) lacked fiscal knowledge 3) opposed the power of Eastern banks 4) were influenced by the silver mining interests.**

______ **2. One explanation of the chronic indebtedness of the western farmers after the Civil War was that 1) they couldn't manage their money 2) their interest rates were exorbitant 3) the cost of agricultural equipment had greatly increased 4) the farmer had to pay high prices for his land.**

_____ 3. One difficulty of the farmer in the post-Civil War period was 1) low tariffs which hurt the farmers 2) Indian raids which destroyed crops 3) worldwide overproduction of agricultural staples 4) the lack of adequate farm labor at harvest time.

_____ 4. As farm prices tended to fall farmers usually 1) curtailed production 2) increased production 3) were able to obtain better credit terms 4) agitated for higher tariff rates.

_____ 5. The Farmers' Alliances believed that the best solution to the farmers' problems was 1) government ownership of the railroads 2) the printing of greenbacks 3) the establishment of collective farms 4) action by the federal government in behalf of the farmer.

_____ 6. Much of the strength of the National Labor Union was lost because 1) of the inadequate leadership of William H. Sylvis 2) it failed to organize on a national scale 3) it failed to back the eight-hour day 4) its efforts were diverted to futile political ends.

_____ 7. The Knights of Labor 1) were the first national labor union 2) appealed especially to the craftsmen 3) foreshadowed the industrial unionism of the twentieth century 4) emphasized the use of terrorism to accomplish its aims.

_____ 8. The American Federation of Labor 1) rejected the basic tenets of capitalism 2) accepted the basic tenets of capitalism 3) sought to bring all of labor into one giant organization 4) was very radical in its initial demands.

_____ 9. The railway strike of 1877 arose 1) out of a dispute over collective bargaining 2) out of the attempt of the A. F. of L. to organize the railroad workers 3) out of an effort of labor leaders to test their strength 4) in protest against a wage cut.

_____ 10. The Pullman strike 1) was a major victory for the workers 2) grew out of the attempts of Eugene Debs to take over the labor movement 3) was proof that the federal government was on the side of labor 4) was a complete defeat for labor.

Essay Questions:

1. What were the basic factors causing the problems of the farmer between 1880 and 1896? Why was it so much more difficult for the farmer to regulate his production than for the businessman?

2. Why did the farmers try to tamper with the currency as a way out of their dilemma?

3. What were the basic origins of the Populist movement?

4. Why were unions an inevitable part of industrialism?

5. Discuss the origins of the National Labor Union and the Knights of Labor. What kept these unions from being successful?

6. How was the American Federation of Labor different from other unions of the nineteenth century? To what did it owe its success?

7. Describe the major strikes of the late nineteenth century. Why were the unions unsuccessful in the struggle for their objectives?

Terms, Events, and Personalities to Know:

Eugene V. Debs	**Haymarket Square**
Pullman	**John P. Altgeld**
Terence V. Powderly	**William H. Sylvis**
Homestead	**Pinkerton**
Samuel Gompers	

CHAPTER VI

The Changing Pattern of American Life

Summary:

A significant by-product of the growth of industry was a rapid increase in the size of the American city. Numerous inventions and technological advances contributed to the rise of the city and in turn were stimulated by the pressing needs created by rapid urban growth. Improved means of rapid transportation, lighting, and even the first of the labor-saving devices were brought into being. The cities, unfortunately, presented a sharp contrast between the world of fashion in which the wealthy lived and the squalid slums of the urban poor. This unfortunate situation was not without its critics. Numerous individuals, such as Jane Addams, helped to bring changes into the municipal situation. The concentration in the great urban centers led to significant changes in the American cultural pattern. Spectator sports came into prominence, enabling the city dweller to obtain enjoyment by watching the games. The concentration of people also made mass education feasible. The expansion of education created larger markets for books, magazines, and newspapers, and the production of such items was vastly increased.

Multiple Choice Questions:

_____ 1. An outstanding aspect of the changes taking place in America after the Civil War was the growth of 1) the influence of the farm community 2) urbanization 3) spiritual values 4) reform impulses from the federal government.

_____ 2. Immigrants from northwestern Europe largely settled in 1) the coal mining areas 2) the prairie states 3) the West coast 4) the large Eastern cities.

_____ 3. The "new immigration" of the late nineteenth century came mainly from 1) the Orient 2) northwestern Europe 3) France 4) southern and eastern Europe.

_____ 4. Julia Lathrop was associated with 1) the campaign for women's rights 2) the temperance movement 3) Hull House 4) the work of the Salvation Army.

_____ 5. The educational institution which grew most rapidly between 1870 and 1900 was the 1) graduate school 2) university 3) kindergarten 4) high school.

_____ 6. The new cities of the era were characterized by 1) uniform prosperity 2) the absence of immigrants 3) a declining standard of living 4) ostentatious wealth and grinding poverty.

_____ 7. An author who sought to instill the basic virtues of American life in the minds of young American boys was 1) Ned Buntline 2) Horatio Alger 3) Henry James 4) Phineas T. Barnum.

_____ 8. Hearst and Pulitzer helped 1) raise the standards of the journalistic world 2) make the newspaper acceptable to the intellectual 3) make journalism profitable for the first time 4) make newspapers acceptable to the great mass of people.

Essay Questions:

1. What contributed to the drift toward the cities during the second half of the nineteenth century?

2. Why did the United States lead in technical innovations?

3. Compare and contrast the living conditions of the wealthy and the urban poor.

4. How did the new immigration differ from the earlier immigration before the Civil War? What problems did the new immigration bring to the United States?

5. With all of the opposition to the new immigration, why was there little or no attempt to halt the flood of immigrants into the country?

6. What attempts were made to improve life in the city from 1880 to 1900?

7. What factors caused the changing patterns of recreation and amusements?

8. How has the changing status of women exercised a profound effect on American life?

9. What changes were taking place in American education in the post-Civil War era? Was the rapid increase in the numbers of those attending school a good omen for the nation or was it harmful?

10. How did the reading habits of the American people reflect the cultural level of the times?

Terms, Events, and Personalities to Know:

Morrill Act	**Joseph Pulitzer**
Anti-Saloon League	**"Mr. Dooley"**
Horatio Alger	**Jacob Riis**
Jane Addams	**John A. Roebling**

CHAPTER VII

Literary and Intellectual Trends

Summary:

The leading post-Civil War literary figure was Walt Whitman. More than any other writer he was able to capture the spirit of the newly emerging America. Another outstanding poet was Emily Dickinson. Mark Twain, with his gusto and humor, mirrored some of the cross currents of American life. William Dean Howells introduced a new note of realism into his own novels and influenced a whole school of writers interested in depicting American life as it was.

The intellectual scene was dominated by the theory of evolution. No area of thought was untouched by it. Conventional religious ideas were challenged, and a new approach to philosophy called pragmatism emerged. The application of evolution to society and business was termed Social Darwinism. This idea was used to fortify laissez-faire concepts and became popular with many Americans. However, there were many critics of Social Darwinism who recommended solutions of their own.

Multiple Choice Questions:

______ **1. The most authentic spokesman of the post-Civil War literary world was 1) Thomas Bailey Aldrich 2) Edwin Markham 3) Stephen Crane 4) Walt Whitman.**

______ **2. The American writer who was best able to catch the spirit of the American frontier was 1) Walt Whitman 2) Mark Twain 3) William Dean Howells 4) Henry James.**

______ 3. In his poetry Edwin Markham was most concerned about 1) a realistic portrayal of farm life 2) the lack of religious impulses 3) the exploitation of labor 4) depicting the adjustment of a soldier on the front lines.

______ 4. In his novels William Dean Howells was most concerned with 1) the abuses under the capitalistic system 2) frontier life 3) the more pleasant aspects of American life 4) Midwestern farm life.

______ 5. The harshness of life on the Midwestern farm was the dominant theme in the writings of 1) Hamlin Garland 2) Stephen Crane 3) Jack London 4) Upton Sinclair.

______ 6. The American graduate schools which rose to prominence after the Civil War were most influenced by the universities of 1) England 2) France 3) Germany 4) Russia.

______ 7. Conventional religious thought was most directly upset by 1) the growth of pragmatism 2) the theory of evolution 3) the development of a materialistic outlook 4) the growth of textual criticism.

______ 8. Which of the following writers was least in sympathy with the viewpoints of the other three? 1) Herbert Spencer 2) John Fiske 3) Lester Ward 4) William Graham Sumner.

______ 9. Henry George is normally associated with 1) demands for a Utopian society 2) Social Darwinism 3) the defense of the Gospel of Wealth 4) the single tax.

______ 10. The philosophy of William James was most concerned with 1) abstractions 2) facts and action 3) fixed principles 4) Thomism.

Essay Questions:

1. To what extent was Walt Whitman "the most authentic spokesman of the new America"?

2. Why was Mark Twain described as "the Lincoln of our literature"?

3. What was the nature of the realism stressed by William Dean Howells? How did his work influence American literature?

4. Why did Darwin's theories have such an impact upon American thought? What was Social Darwinism?

5. What were the basic tenets of pragmatism?

6. Upon what basis was American society criticized in the latter decades of the nineteenth century? Describe the attacks of George, Bellamy, Lloyd, and Ward.

Terms, Events, and Personalities to Know:

Henry James	**Emily Dickinson**
Main-Travelled Roads	**Frank Norris**
William Graham Sumner	**Edwin Markham**
Thomas Bailey Aldrich	**Vassar**
Josiah Strong	**Charles W. Eliot**
Progress and Poverty	**William Dean Howells**
Democratic Vistas	**Johns Hopkins**
Stephen Crane	**William James**
Looking Backward	

CHAPTER VIII

The Political Scene

Summary:

In the period between the Civil War and 1896 political democracy was at a low point in American history. Political leadership was mediocre and neither party showed much interest in the good of the nation. In fact, there was virtually no difference between the parties on the issues facing the nation. Dishonesty in government was also nonpartisan. After the nation had weathered two terms with Grant as President, it narrowly missed disaster in the disputed election of 1876.

The first federal civil service act, one of the few constructive pieces of legislation of the period, was passed only after President Garfield's assassination. The election of 1884 was one of personalities, with the people having little opportunity to hear a discussion of the issues. Under Cleveland, the victor in this contest, the tariff emerged as a point of difference between the two parties. Although Cleveland was easily the most competent President of the era he was to be confronted with one of the nation's most critical depressions. In refusing to make economic recovery a matter of concern to the national government, President Cleveland was simply following accepted practice.

Multiple Choice Questions:

_____ 1. The political era between the Civil War and 1896 was characterized by 1) an able exposition of the issues before America 2) a large number of distinguished politicians in both parties 3) a lack of real consideration of the issues before the country 4) strong reformist sentiments.

_____ 2. During the years 1868–96 1) the country was closely divided in its political allegiance 2) the Republicans were undisputed masters in Washington 3) the Democratic party practically ceased to exist 4) the Democrats were never able to control either the House or the Senate.

_____ 3. NOT true of Ulysses S. Grant was that he 1) lacked sound judgment of men 2) was indirect and irresolute where public affairs were concerned 3) was personally involved in some of the grafts during his administration 4) had no real grasp of the problems of the presidency.

_____ 4. The basic mistake of the liberal Republicans in 1872 was 1) their opposition to Grant 2) their failure to fight a spirited campaign 3) their alliance with the Democrats 4) their nomination of Greeley.

_____ 5. In the election of 1876 1) Hayes was clearly the popular favorite 2) the final decision was made by the House 3) Tilden was the popular favorite 4) Tilden had a clear majority in the electoral college.

_____ 6. As a President, Hayes was 1) a dynamic and resourceful leader 2) a distinct improvement over Grant 3) responsible for the continuation of carpetbag rule in the South 4) responsible for soft-money policies.

_____ 7. President Arthur 1) was a much better chief executive than had been expected 2) opened the door to the favoritism of the Grant era 3) was able to obtain tariff reform 4) opposed civil service reform.

_____ 8. James G. Blaine 1) had the backing of the Mugwumps 2) had little popular support within Republican ranks 3) was too ready to sacrifice principle for expediency 4) had few political foes.

_____ 9. In the election of 1888 1) Cleveland had a majority in the electoral college 2) Cleveland had more popular votes than did Harrison 3) Harrison campaigned as a reformist Republican 4) Harrison campaigned as a low tariff candidate.

_____ 10. Cleveland's second administration was marred by 1) personal scandals 2) a party split over the tariff 3) frequent disputes with the Supreme Court 4) a serious downturn in the national economy.

Essay Questions:

1. Why were the Republicans able to dominate national politics between 1865 and 1900?

2. Why was this period in national political life marked by corruption and mediocrity?

3. What factors made Grant, a successful general, such a complete failure as President? Why was he re-elected in 1872 after his incapacity to lead the nation was revealed?

4. Why has the election of 1876 been described as "the most serious challenge American democracy has faced"?

5. To what extent might one argue that the "spoils system" is an essential feature of democracy?

6. James G. Blaine was the outstanding politician of his era. Why, then, did he fail to be elected to the presidency?

7. Cleveland's election was hailed as a national disaster by the Republicans. Why did his election make little difference in national politics?

8. Discuss the controversy over civil service, tariff, and currency reform.

9. What caused the panic of 1893?

Terms, Events, and Personalities to Know:

Bland-Allison Act
Halfbreeds
Horatio Seymour
"Mugwumps"
McKinley Act
Roscoe Conkling
Samuel J. Tilden
Whiskey Ring
Pendleton Act
Wilson-Gorman Act
Stalwarts
"Plumed Knight"

CHAPTER IX

Populism and the Election of 1896

Summary:

The tide of agrarian and labor discontent which had been rising steadily erupted in the election of 1896. Populism, a movement born of desperation, attempted to assert the rights of the producing classes and break the hold of monopoly capitalism. The movement had a broad base of support among the people of the West and the South and an able, if eccentric, group of leaders. William Jennings Bryan accepted major aims of the Populists and made their program that of the Democratic party despite the opposition of President Cleveland and the Eastern wing of the party. The most important Populist objective was currency inflation through the free coinage of silver. The Republican presidential candidate was William McKinley, but their real leader was Mark Hanna. Bryan was depicted as a revolutionist who would bring a reign of terror to America. McKinley captured the election by carrying the Eastern states.

Multiple Choice Questions:

_____ 1. To the Populists, the number one enemy of the nation was 1) gold 2) the Eastern industrialists 3) the railways 4) the free coinage of silver.

_____ 2. Most of the men and women who led the Populist movement were from 1) Minnesota 2) Iowa 3) Kansas 4) South Carolina.

_____ 3. The key to the great popularity of William Jennings Bryan lay in 1) the soundness of his grasp of economic and social issues 2) his craftiness as a politician 3) his intellectual depth 4) his ability to express the feelings of rural Midwestern America.

_____ 4. The direction of the Republican campaign in 1896 was mainly in the hands of 1) Mark Hanna 2) Theodore Roosevelt 3) William McKinley 4) James G. Blaine.

_____ 5. The fundamental issue in the election of 1896 was 1) Bryan's ability to lead the national effectively 2) the Populist attempt to accomplish a social revolution 3) a clash between the old agrarian order and the new capitalist economy 4) whether or not the safeguards in the Constitution could be retained.

_____ 6. The Democrat-Populist platform of 1896 called for all of the following with the exception of 1) more effective regulation of the railroads 2) an income tax 3) more stringent laws to regulate the trusts 4) a social security law.

_____ 7. As President, William McKinley 1) was a dynamic and popular leader 2) was prepared to ask for much reform legislation to aid the farmers 3) lacked the essential qualities of effective leadership 4) brought little dignity to the White House.

_____ 8. It is obvious from his poetry that Vachel Lindsay 1) did not approve of the aims of the Populists 2) regretted the defeat of Bryan 3) was a personal friend of William McKinley 4) supported the gold standard.

_____ 9. Judging by the election results in 1896 Bryan 1) failed to carry even the Deep South 2) failed to carry the mining states of the West 3) failed to win much support in the Northeast 4) lacked the backing of even the prairie farming states.

_____ 10. There was less demand for the free coinage of silver after 1896 because 1) the free silverites lost in 1896 3) the sixteen to one ratio was proven to be unsound 3) Britain went off the gold standard 4) returning prosperity and new gold discoveries caused a rise in prices.

Essay Questions:

1. **Account for the tremendous popularity of the Populist movement.**
2. **Who were the principal leaders of the Populists? Why do you suppose the movement attracted so many eccentrics?**
3. **Why did the Populist movement reach its height in 1896?**
4. **What was the secret of the political appeal of William Jennings Bryan? How could Bryan be said to have represented the strength and the weakness of rural Midwestern America?**
5. **It has been said that the Democratic-Populist coalition may have "lost the battle in 1896 but ultimately won the war." Discuss the implications of this quote.**
6. **Why did the McKinley election bring relative quiet to the political arena?**

Terms, Events, and Personalities to Know:

Dingley Tariff
"Cross of Gold"
"Pitchfork Ben" Tillman
Mark Hanna
Mary Ellen Lease
"Sage of Nininger"
"Sockless Jerry" Simpson
General James B. Weaver
"Bloody Bridles" Waite
William A. Peffer

CHAPTER X

Imperialism

Summary:

Expansion has always played a significant role in American history. Once the frontier was settled it was perhaps inevitable that the nation should expand overseas. The acquisition of Alaska was the first move in this pattern. By the 1890's proponents of American involvement overseas contended that because our economy had matured, it was our duty to extend the benefits of our civilization to backward people. Moreover, our defense made expansion necessary. Captain Alfred Thayer Mahan was the foremost exponent of the defense thesis.

Within a few years the United States emerged as the protector of Latin America and with heavy commitments in the Orient. These new responsibilities were resisted by many Americans as unnecessary. Others simply resented the expense caused by having to protect holdings and investments in the far corners of the world and yearned for a simpler age.

Multiple Choice Questions:

_____ **1. The main accomplishment of the Treaty of Washington was 1) the settling of the fisheries question 2) the settling of the Samoan Islands controversy 3) the submitting of the "Alabama" claims to arbitration 4) the agreement to annex Santo Domingo.**

_____ **2. Alfred Thayer Mahan is most frequently associated with 1) the frontier theme in American history 2) the justification of imperialism on the grounds of duty 3) American interest in the Hawaiian Islands 4) the belief that sea power was the most important element in national defense.**

_____ **3. In the Venezuelan dispute of 1895, Secretary of State Olney 1) cautiously defended the Monroe Doctrine 2) militantly pronounced the American position in the Western Hemisphere 3) openly sought war with Britain 4) showed that the Cleveland administration was very pro-British.**

_____ **4. In handling the dispute in Hawaii in 1893 President Cleveland did all of the following EXCEPT 1) withdraw the treaty of annexation from the Senate 2) recognize the formal independence of the Republic of Hawaii 3) restore Queen Liliuokalani to her throne 4) allow the revolutionary government in Hawaii to remain in power.**

_____ **5. The Spanish-American War was mainly caused by 1) President McKinley's keen desire for war 2) the clamor of the American businessmen for war 3) irresponsible journalism 4) Spain's unwillingness to meet American demands in Cuba.**

_____ **6. In general, the Filipinos wanted to 1) accept American rule 2) become independent 3) remain under Spanish rule 4) accept German rule.**

_____ **7. Which of the following was NOT a direct result of the Spanish-American War? 1) Puerto Rico was annexed. 2) Cuba became a thinly disguised American protectorate. 3) the Philippines were annexed. 4) Cuba was annexed.**

_____ **8. The Hay Open Door Policy 1) was enacted to save China after the Boxer Rebellion 2) was promptly accepted by Japan 3) insisted upon trade equality and respect for China's sovereignty 4) kept the United States from being involved in China's affairs.**

______ 9. What part of America's imperialistic ventures was most unpopular at the time of its acquisition? 1) annexation of Hawaii 2) the purchase of Louisiana 3) the annexation of the Philippines 4) the annexation of Puerto Rico.

______ 10. In 1946 the United States granted to which of its former colonies complete independence? 1) Cuba 2) Puerto Rico 3) Alaska 4) The Philippines.

Essay Questions:

1. Why did the post-Civil War period in American history become "the nadir of diplomacy"? What was the nature of the diplomacy of the period?

2. What prompted the nation to look outward in the 1890's?

3. What were the basic ideas of the Mahan school of expansionism? Do you believe their motives have been proved sound? Argue both sides of this point.

4. What was the Venezuela crisis of 1895? Why did it have a significant influence on American foreign policy?

5. Discuss the causes of the Spanish-American War. Was the United States justified in going to war?

6. What were the long-range effects of the Spanish-American War?

7. Why was there so much controversy over the annexation of the Philippines? What groups supported annexation? Which groups were opposed to annexation?

8. Describe the basis of America's interest in the Far East. What was the Hay Open Door Policy?

Terms, Events, and Personalities to Know:

Insular Cases
"Rough Riders"
"Alabama Claims"
Boxers
"Butcher" Weyler
Albert J. Beveridge
Pago Pago
"Seward's Folly"
"full dinner pail"
Queen Liliuokalani
Tydings-McDuffie Act
Emilio Aguinaldo
British Guiana
Jones Act
Platt Amendment
Treaty of Washington

Map Exercise I

Locate the following:

1. The route of the proposed Nicaragua Canal
2. The route of the Panama Canal
3. The area involved in the Venezuela Controversy of 1895
4. Santo Domingo
5. Haiti
6. Puerto Rico
7. Honduras
8. Vera Cruz

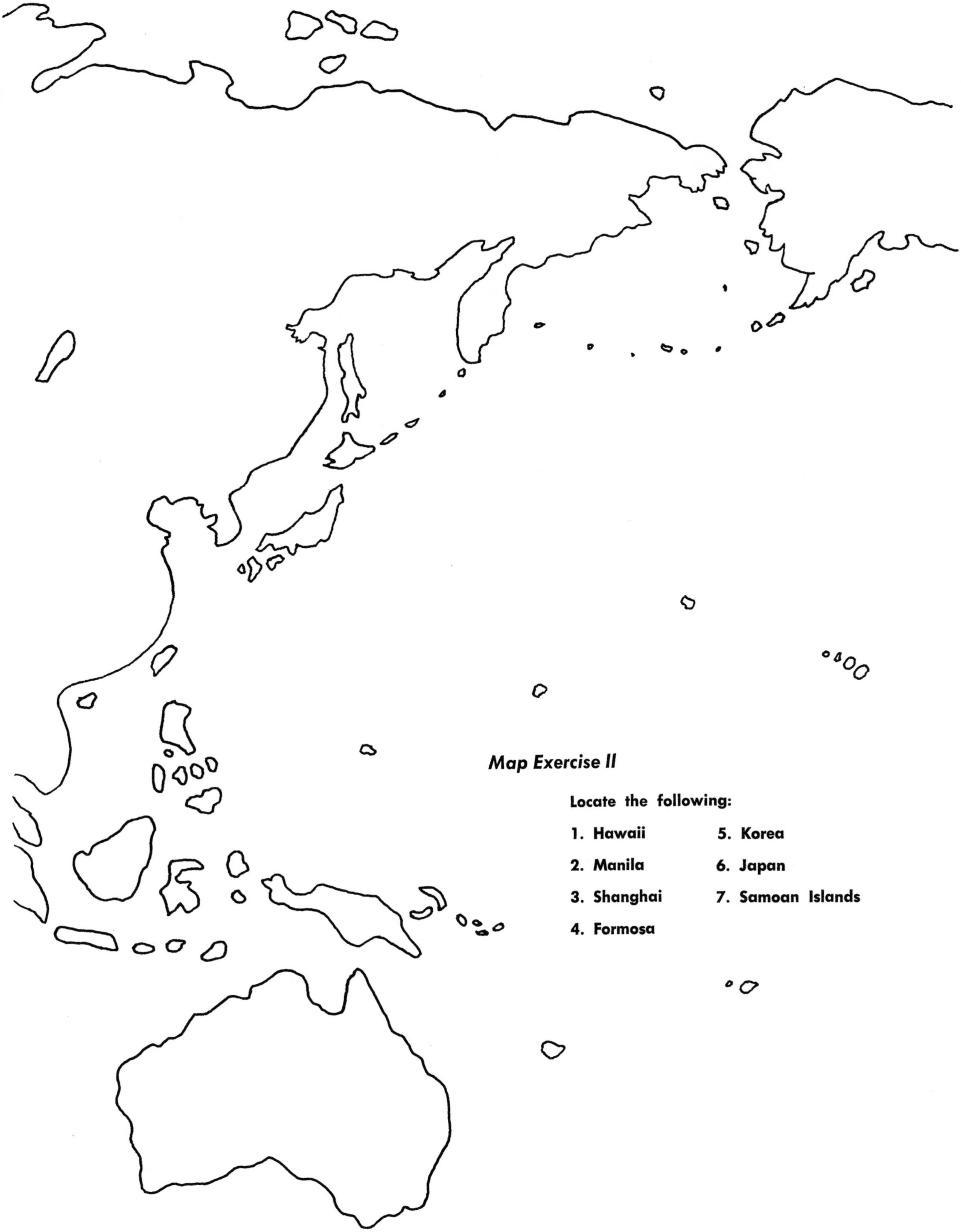

Map Exercise II

Locate the following:

1. **Hawaii**
2. **Manila**
3. **Shanghai**
4. **Formosa**
5. **Korea**
6. **Japan**
7. **Samoan Islands**

CHAPTER XI

The Spirit of Progressivism

Summary:

Progressivism was a many-sided attack upon evils which had developed in America. Unlike most reform movements it arose at a time of optimism and prosperity instead of at a time of despair and depression. The leaders of this movement were among the nation's most substantial citizens and included Presidents Theodore Roosevelt and Wilson. Professional journalists, dubbed muckrakers, helped stir interest in reform. The Progressives were to be found in both political parties and had no separate organization. They were bound together in a common effort to eliminate the most glaring abuses of unbridled laissez faire. In short, they wanted to adjust urban-industrial America to the ideals of a rural-agrarian society. They worked through local, state, and national governments in their efforts to make the nation's political institutions more responsive to the will of the people. For better or worse Progressivism has deeply influenced twentieth-century America.

Multiple Choice Questions:

______ 1. The Progressive era dates from 1) 1896 2) Wilson's inaugural address 3) the moment Roosevelt took office 4) the formation of the National Progressive Republican League.

______ 2. The best explanation as to why Progressivism succeeded and Populism failed is that the former was 1) much more radical in nature 2) a movement that placed more emphasis upon panaceas than did Populism 3) a movement that had more support from distressed farmers 4) able to obtain a broader base of support.

______ 3. Which of the following should NOT be classed as a Progressive? 1) Albert Beveridge 2) George F. Baer 3) William Allen White 4) Tom Johnson.

______ 4. The evils which the Progressives sought to correct were first called to the nation's attention by 1) professional journalists 2) labor critics 3) professional politicians 4) distressed farmers.

______ 5. Which of the following muckrakers is improperly associated? 1) Lincoln Steffens—the failure of city government 2) Burton J. Hendrick—fraud and corruption in the Senate 3) Ray Stannard Baker—the wrongdoing of the railroads 4) Ida Tarbell—an exposé of Rockefeller's business practices.

______ 6. A muckraking novel that directly influenced the passage of the federal meat inspection act was 1) *The Octopus* 2) *The Titan* 3) *Mr. Crewe's Career* 4) *The Jungle.*

______ 7. The leading states in passing Progressive legislation were 1) Kansas and California 2) Oregon and Wisconsin 3) Minnesota and New Jersey 4) Iowa and Ohio.

______ 8. Which of the following constitutional amendments was not a result of agitation during the Progressive era? 1) Fifteenth 2) Sixteenth 3) Seventeenth 4) Eighteenth.

______ 9. Helping to retard the enactment of labor legislation during the Progressive era was 1) the indifference of public opinion 2) the opinions of the Supreme Court 3) the failure to get such legislation through Congress 4) the impossibility of enforcing such legislation.

______ 10. In their efforts to preserve the capitalist system the Progressives ultimately came to 1) rely upon free enterprise only 2) rely upon the enactment of state laws 3) rely upon the enactment of national legislation 4) a belief that a certain amount of socialism was necessary.

Essay Questions:

1. What were the basic philosophical tenets of Progressivism? What were the objectives of the Progressives?

2. Who were the leading muckrakers? To what extent were they indispensable to the Progressive movement?

3. What were the reform attempts of the movement on the local level? How successful was this effort?

4. Why were the direct election of United States senators and woman suffrage such an integral part of the reform movement?

5. How did the judiciary respond to the Progressive movement?

Terms, Events, and Personalities to Know:

Herbert Croly
"Fighting Bob" La Follette
Eugene V. Debs
Adkins v *Children's Hospital*
Ida Tarbell
Nineteenth Amendment
The Treason of the Senate
Lochner v *New York*
"muckrakers"
"the great dissenter"
The Jungle
Ray Stannard Baker
Burton J. Hendrick
Thorstein Veblen
The Octopus
Seventeenth Amendment
Lincoln Steffens

CHAPTER XII

The Roosevelt Era

Summary:

Theodore Roosevelt was the most dynamic and colorful President America had had in many years. To many Americans he personified the government. Taking over the White House in September 1901, Roosevelt gave to the Progressive movement valuable leadership. Essentially a conservative, he became a reformer because he was a perceptive politician who understood what the people wanted. Although he broke few trusts, he earned a reputation as a trustbuster. In a national coal strike Roosevelt intervened in the public interest, the first President to act in this position. Of the regulatory measures passed during his administration the most significant concerned conservation.

William Howard Taft, Roosevelt's hand-picked successor, was not suited to the political leadership required of a President. Although he was a good administrator and had a fair record of reform, the Republican party split under Taft. In 1912 Roosevelt sought to regain the White House, and when Taft defeated him for the GOP nomination he organized a third party. This may have aided in the election of Woodrow Wilson in 1912.

Multiple Choice Questions:

______ 1. As President, Theodore Roosevelt 1) had a coherent reform program 2) gave the country the leadership it had lacked 3) was too much a politician to sponsor constructive legislation 4) fought tenaciously for a wide variety of reforms.

______ 2. Theodore Roosevelt was characterized by all BUT one of the following, he: 1) had much confidence in his own ability 2) approached the powers of the presidency as a strong leader 3) had a cold and unappealing personality 4) brought to the White House a background of varied experiences.

______ 3. In his attitude toward the trusts Roosevelt 1) tried to make a distinction between good and bad trusts 2) attempted to break up all large business combines 3) was too close to the business community to attack the trusts effectively 4) had new laws passed to strengthen the Sherman Anti-Trust Act.

______ 4. In his handling of the coal strike of 1902 Roosevelt 1) used troops to break the strike 2) completely backed the position of the union 3) established a precedent by intervening in a strike in the public interest 4) followed the advice of J. P. Morgan.

______ 5. Which of the following was NOT true of the 1904 election? 1) Roosevelt was the first Vice-President to be elected in his own right who had gone to the White House through the death of the President. 2) The Democrats hoped to capitalize on Roosevelt's supposed antagonism toward business. 3) Roosevelt met little opposition to his renomination within Republican ranks. 4) The election was another defeat for Bryan.

______ 6. The Hepburn Act 1) provided for federal meat inspection 2) greatly strengthened the Interstate Commerce Commission 3) made it easier to prosecute the larger trusts 4) established a commission to arbitrate labor disputes.

______ 7. One area in which President Roosevelt made a lasting contribution concerned 1) setting the Republican party on a liberal path 2) stressing the importance of conserving the nation's resources 3) abolishing child labor 4) stressing that the powers of the federal government must not be expanded.

______ 8. As President, Taft 1) lacked administrative ability 2) tended to be too radical 3) tried to divorce the policies of his administration from those of Roosevelt's 4) lacked the ability to dramatize his accomplishments.

______ 9. In bidding for the Republican presidential nomination in 1912 Roosevelt, in addition to challenging Taft, had to challenge another Progressive named 1) Charles Evans Hughes 2) Elihu Root 3) Albert J. Beveridge 4) Robert M. La Follette.

______ 10. In the election of 1912 it was apparent that 1) it is easy to launch successful political parties 2) Wilson was a successful vote-getter 3) the voters preferred a more liberal candidate than President Taft 4) the platforms of the Democrats and the Progressives were identical.

Essay Questions:

1. Evaluate the talents of Theodore Roosevelt as President. To what extent did he come to personify the Progressive movement? How did his concept of the Presidency differ from that of McKinley and other nineteenth-century presidents?

2. How successful was Roosevelt in his attack upon the trusts? Why was the attack not more successful than it was?

3. What was the long-range significance of Roosevelt's interference in the coal strike of 1902?

4. Many historians contend that Roosevelt's most lasting contribution was in the field of conservation. Describe his work in this area.

5. Compare and contrast the basic features of Taft's administration with that of Roosevelt. Why did Taft have so much difficulty as President?

6. Why has the election of 1912 generally been regarded as one of the most significant in American history? Discuss the basic problems of this election. What were the long-range effects of the results?

Terms, Events, and Personalities to Know:

Bull Moose
Joseph Cannon
Alton B. Parker
Champ Clark
Inland Waterways Commission
Northern Securities Case
Osawatomie speech
Pure Food and Drug Act
Gifford Pinchot
Hepburn Act
Payne-Aldrich Tariff
George F. Baer
Mann-Elkins Act
John Mitchell

CHAPTER XIII

The New Freedom

Summary:

During the first administration of Woodrow Wilson the Progressive movement came to full maturity. The new President accepted the basic objectives of Progressivism and desired to reconstruct society in order to restore for individual Americans the freedom that had been submerged by a ruthless economic system. This was to be accomplished by a series of laws. With the Democrats in control of both houses of Congress, Wilson had no difficulty in getting laws passed which lowered the tariffs, restrained trusts, established a new national banking system, and materially improved the positions of both farmers and labor. By the conclusion of the first Wilson administration most of the objectives of the Progressives had been enacted into law.

Multiple Choice Questions:

______ 1. When it came to using the powers of the presidency to accomplish his objectives the views of Woodrow Wilson were most similar to those of 1) William Howard Taft 2) Theodore Roosevelt 3) William McKinley 4) Benjamin Harrison.

______ 2. Woodrow Wilson's political philosophy was characterized by 1) an intense desire to reform America along socialistic lines 2) deference to the leadership of Congress 3) an abounding faith in the basic precepts of American democracy 4) a firm belief that those who possessed wealth should govern.

______ 3. In his rise to the presidency all of the following were true of Wilson EXCEPT that 1) his background had been academic rather than legal 2) his Calvinist faith gave him a strong belief in principles 3) he had not always been known for his progressive views 4) like Chester Arthur he had always worked closely with the leaders of his party.

______ 4. Wilson first demanded reform of 1) the tariff 2) currency 3) trust regulation 4) the rights of labor.

______ 5. Which of the following was NOT true of the Federal Reserve Act? 1) It provided for greater elasticity of the currency. 2) It preserved private banking under governmental control. 3) It was generally successful in promoting financial stability. 4) It established a system of private control of national banking.

______ 6. As compared to the Sherman Anti-Trust Act the Clayton Act 1) was more general in nature 2) was not much more successful when it came to controlling trusts 3) placed more emphasis on breaking trusts and less on regulation 4) permitted interlocking directorates in competing corporations.

______ 7. When Samuel Gompers spoke of "Labor's Charter of Freedom" he had reference to the 1) Adamson Act 2) Norris-La Guardia Act 3) Clayton Act 4) La Follette Seamen's Act.

______ 8. The Pujo Committee 1) revealed shocking abuses of child labor 2) brought reforms in rural credit 3) recommended an income tax 4) revealed that the nation's finances were controlled by a few men.

Essay Questions:

1. Many American historians have selected Woodrow Wilson as one of our "great" Presidents. Why do you suppose they have so honored Wilson? How was he well qualified to be President?

2. How did the Underwood Tariff constitute a victory for Wilson? What was unique about this tariff bill?

3. Discuss the main features of Wilson's attempt at monetary reform. How does the Federal Reserve System work?

4. Why was Wilson's attempt to control the trusts the least successful part of his legislative program?

5. What steps were taken by the Wilson Administration to aid labor? How successful were they?

Terms, Events, and Personalities to Know:

"Labor's Charter of Freedom"
Pujo Committee
Child Labor Act
"cease and desist"
La Follette Seamen's Act
Federal Farm Loan Act
Adamson Act
Clayton Act
Federal Trade Commission

CHAPTER XIV

Social and Cultural Change

Summary:

The beginning of the twentieth century in America was characterized by great changes. Numerous inventions spurred technological advance, which aided the growth of the cities. Social, economic, and cultural patterns were much altered.

Organized labor made some gains in the period preceding World War I, with the conservative A. F. of L. being more important than the radical I.W.W. Immigration continued to bring workmen to America faster than society could absorb them. The aliens, largely from southern and eastern Europe, settled in the larger cities. The status of the immigrant in America was similar to that of the Negro. The prohibition movement was related to the desire of many to protect the Negro and the immigrant from the evils of alcohol.

The coming of the automobile and the introduction of the movies had a considerable impact on American society. The popular literature of the early 1900's was sentimental but enjoyed very large sales. More serious writers fared less well. American art and architecture sought to be free of dependence on Europe, and architecture was probably most successful in the development of a native style.

Multiple Choice Questions:

______ 1. The changing tempo of life at the beginning of the twentieth century was NOT marked by 1) revolutionary technological changes 2) a marked change in the way of life in rural America 3) significant discoveries in the field of medicine 4) a distinct change in the way of life of urban America.

______ 2. The A. F. of L. exhibited little interest in 1) trying to end the use of injunctions in labor disputes 2) the outlawing of yellow dog contracts 3) supporting any political candidates 4) organizing mass production industries.

______ 3. Which of the following was NOT true of the I.W.W.? 1) It attracted much support from members of the A. F. of L. 2) Its membership never exceeded sixty thousand. 3) Its goal was to do away with capitalism. 4) It won a textile strike at Lawrence, Massachusetts.

______ 4. One objective of those who favored a literacy test for immigrants was to 1) increase immigration from southern and eastern Europe 2) make available more cheap labor for industry 3) retain America's historic role as the land of opportunity for the masses of Europe 4) encourage immigration from northwestern Europe.

______ 5. In his efforts to improve the position of Negroes, Booker T. Washington was most interested in 1) improving their social position in the South 2) advocating their migration northward 3) improving their economic position 4) obtaining complete political equality.

______ 6. NOT true of the prohibition movement was that 1) it originated in rural America's distrust of the city 2) it grew out of the recognized evils of the saloons 3) it obtained much support from church groups 4) it resulted in lasting reforms.

______ 7. Most directly changing the lives of the American people was the general use of 1) movies 2) airplanes 3) automobiles 4) telephones.

______ 8. The first movie to tell a complete story was 1) *The Perils of Pauline* 2) *The Great Train Robbery* 3) *The Birth of a Nation* 4) *The Wizard of Oz.*

______ 9. Which of the following authors best represented the sentimental literary tastes of the first decade of the twentieth century? 1) Sherwood Anderson 2) Edgar Lee Masters 3) Gene Stratton Porter 4) Jack London.

______ 10. The cultural expression of the United States in the first decade of the century was least important in 1) architecture 2) painting 3) music 4) sculpture.

Essay Questions:

1. Describe the general character of life in the Roosevelt-Wilson era.

2. Compare the methods and objectives of the A. F. of L. with those of the I. W. W.

3. Discuss the arguments for and against the tightening of immigration restrictions.

4. How did the drive for temperance typify the spirit of reform of the early twentieth century?

5. What was the effect of the automobile on the American way of life?

6. How was the growth of the movies a reflection of the quest for a mass culture?

7. What was the basic theme in literature in the period before World War I?

8. Why was American artistic talent to achieve its finest expression in architecture? What were the essential features of this new architecture?

Terms, Events, and Personalities to Know:

Louis Sullivan
Mary Antin
NAACP
Willa Cather
Frank Lloyd Wright
Melting Pot
Webb-Kenyon Act
"Ellis Island art"
The Great Train Robbery
Edwin Arlington Robinson
"Ash Can School"
Henry Pratt Fairchild
The Birth of a Nation
"open shop"
"yellow dog contracts"
Booker T. Washington
John Sloan
William DuBois
Sherwood Anderson
John Marin

CHAPTER XV

The Road to War

Summary:

Between 1900 and its involvement in war in 1917 the nation slowly drifted away from its traditional policy of isolation. The acquisition of the Panama Canal, the announcement of the Roosevelt Corollary to the Monroe Doctrine, and an increase in American investments in northern Latin America committed us to affairs in that area. In an effort to protect our trading rights in China, President Roosevelt helped settle the Russo-Japanese War. Subsequent events led to the emergence of the United States as the defender of China against the aggressive intentions of the Japanese. American participation in the Algeciras Conference further symbolized the drift away from isolation.

American intervention in World War I resulted from our desire to maintain our rights as a neutral while at the same time our factories were supporting the war efforts of England and France. In order to halt the flow of goods to the Allies, Germany violated existing international law in her use of the submarine, thereby drawing the United States into the conflict.

Multiple Choice Questions:

______ 1. President Roosevelt's precipitate action over the Panama Canal resulted from 1) Britain's rejection of the first Hay-Pauncefote Treaty 2) Colombia's rejection of the Hay-Herran Treaty 3) his interest in obtaining the independence of Panama 4) Congressional support of the Nicaraguan site.

______ 2. Which of the following Caribbean nations had NOT become a virtual protectorate of the United States by 1916? 1) Nicaragua 2) Guatemala 3) Panama 4) Haiti.

______ 3. The Roosevelt Corollary to the Monroe Doctrine was intended to 1) keep Germany out of the Caribbean 2) justify United States seizure of Panama 3) justify United States intervention in the Caribbean 4) make Latin American nations partners in interpreting the Monroe Doctrine.

______ 4. Most Latin Americans interpreted the Caribbean policy of Roosevelt and Taft as 1) a friendly gesture of a big brother 2) a sincere effort to protect their own best interests 3) a prelude to actual annexation by the United States 4) imperialism hidden under a principle of international law.

______ 5. The rivalry between the United States and Japan in the Orient 1) started when Hay announced his Open Door Policy 2) dates from the Treaty of Portsmouth 3) grew out of Japanese resentment over the Gentlemen's Agreement 4) grew out of the American annexation of the Philippines.

______ 6. The Algeciras Conference of 1906 1) revealed the growing rift between Germany on the one hand and England and France on the other 2) was a wanton example of American intervention in African affairs 3) was an example of Roosevelt's intention to uphold the Monroe Doctrine 4) was a repudiation of Roosevelt's attempt to be a peacemaker.

______ 7. Wilson's refusal to recognize the Huerta government in Mexico was based upon 1) traditional American recognition policies 2) a desire to protect American oil interests in Mexico 3) fear of British influence upon Huerta 4) a moralistic interpretation of the issues.

______ 8. The basic quarrel between the United States and Germany between 1914 and 1917 grew out of 1) America's close friendship with Britain 2) Germany's desire to use the submarine to cut off supplies to Britain 3) Germany's intervention in Mexico 4) British propaganda that portrayed the Germans in the most cruel way.

______ 9. In the election of 1916 the pivotal state was 1) New Jersey 2) New York 3) Wisconsin 4) California.

______ 10. President Wilson justified his demand for a declaration of war on the grounds that 1) the Zimmerman note was a threat to national security 2) war was necessary to protect American loans to the Allies 3) the German government was making war on the United States 4) a German victory over the Allies would make America's position untenable.

Essay Questions:

1. How did the United States acquire the right to build the Panama Canal?
2. What was "Dollar Diplomacy"? How did the Roosevelt Corollary bolster American foreign policy in the Caribbean?
3. How did Roosevelt's policy toward the Latin American countries cause friction between the United States and the area south of the Rio Grande?
4. Why did the American role at the Treaty of Portsmouth cause friction between the United States and Japan?
5. What was the basis of Wilson's policy toward the Huerta government of Mexico? Was this policy justified?
6. To what extent did the United States fail to maintain strict neutrality in the period between 1914 and 1917? Did the American sale of war goods to the Allies justify Germany's submarine warfare?
7. How did the economic situation help decide America to enter the war on the side of the Allies? Why was this only a part of the reason for America's decision to fight Germany?
8. Why were most Americans inclined to favor the British position over that of the Germans?

Terms, Events, and Personalities to Know:

Zimmerman note
"watchful waiting"
Charles Evans Hughes
"peace without victory"
Victoriano Huerta
Edward M. House

Hay-Pauncefote Treaty
"missionary diplomacy"
Twenty-One Demands
de facto recognition
Algeciras Conference
"Lusitania"

CHAPTER XVI

The Great Crusade

Summary:

The American people quickly proved capable of organizing for war. To meet the tremendous expenses of war, taxes were increased and large amounts were borrowed through bond issues. The nation submitted to a degree of control over industry, agriculture, and labor unheard of in a free society. Most people willingly supported the war effort but, unfortunately, those who did not were harassed in a manner that ill-suited the world's greatest democracy.

An American army was raised, equipped, and transported to Europe in time to play a decisive role in the ultimate victory. Once the war was won, President Wilson attempted to write a peace treaty based on his idealistic Fourteen Points. The American leader was forced to make many concessions to his European allies, who were mainly interested in punishing Germany. However, the treaty which emerged was reasonably fair. Unfortunately, a United States disillusioned with the results of the "Great Crusade" turned away from Europe and rejected the Versailles Treaty and membership in the League of Nations created by the President.

Multiple Choice Questions:

_____ **1. During World War I the economy on the home front was controlled mainly by 1) strict rationing and price controls 2) a total mobilization of the nation's labor force 3) the government's taking over agriculture and industry 4) appeals for voluntary co-operation.**

_____ **2. America's war effort was marked by 1) numerous strikes sponsored by the A. F. of L. 2) widespread interference with civil liberties 3) a lack of public support for the war 4) a failure to inform the public concerning American war aims.**

_____ **3. Which of the following was NOT true of the American Expeditionary Force? 1) It was commanded by John J. Pershing. 2) Though organized hastily and ill-trained it fought well. 3) Over a million troops saw action on the front. 4) The A.E.F. was used only to bolster the French and British armies and did not fight as a separate unit.**

_____ 4. NOT true of the American Navy in the war was that 1) it aided in the creation of an effective convoy system 2) it played a most insignificant role in the war effort 3) it helped the British lay the North Sea mine barrage 4) it performed outstanding service in helping to control the submarine menace.

_____ 5. Of all of the Fourteen Points the most significant to Wilson was the one concerning 1) freedom of the seas 2) self-determination of peoples 3) an association of nations to maintain the peace 4) the removal of artificial trade barriers.

_____ 6. The most grievous error of the peacemakers at Versailles was their failure to 1) pay any attention to the self-determination principle that Wilson had stressed 2) make Germany admit her war guilt 3) force Germany to pay adequate reparations 4) consider properly the economic aspects of international relations.

_____ 7. The Treaty of Versailles 1) forced Germany to pay an established amount in reparations 2) was a harsher treaty than Germany would have enacted had she been the victor 3) was a milder treaty than a victorious Germany would have demanded 4) acceded to French demands that Germany be dismembered.

_____ 8. Wilson's basic failure at the peace conference was 1) his willingness to make compromises 2) his assumption that the American people were ready for international obligations 3) his failure to take leading Republicans to the conference 4) the result of his demand for a Democratic Congress in 1918.

_____ 9. The Versailles Treaty more than likely could have been ratified in the Senate 1) if Wilson had been willing to accept Lodge's reservations 2) if Wilson had not suffered a physical collapse 3) if the Democratic senators had not deserted the President 4) if Wilson had been less willing to compromise with his political foes.

_____ 10. In the election of 1920 1) the Democrats made League membership the main campaign issue 2) the Republicans came out against any form of international cooperation 3) the Republicans won a very narrow victory 4) most voters were keenly interested in the issue of League membership.

Essay Questions:

1. How was the home front organized for war production in 1917?
2. Why was there such a widespread suppression of civil liberties in 1917?
3. Why was the participation of the American army decisive in the war on the Western front?
4. What were the essential features of the Fourteen Points?
5. What were the basic problems confronting Wilson at Versailles? To what extent was the Versailles Treaty a success? To what extent was it a failure?
6. What features of the Versailles Treaty were most objectionable to the United States Senate? Why did the Senate reject the treaty?
7. To what extent was the election of 1920 a referendum on American participation in the League? Why did the United States turn toward isolation in the 1920's?

Terms, Events, and Personalities to Know:

James M. Cox
"gasless Sundays"
League Covenant
Somme
George Creel
Henry Cabot Lodge
St. Mihiel
"liberty cabbage"
Lodge Reservations
Meuse-Argonne
Espionage Act
Bernard M. Baruch
A. E. F.
Belgian Relief Commission
Shantung

CHAPTER XVII

Foreign Policy in the 1920's

Summary:

Having been instrumental in rejecting the Versailles Treaty, the Republicans continued to follow an isolationist policy. This pattern was begun by the refusal to accord diplomatic recognition to the Bolshevik regime in Russia. It was continued in the inability of Washington to recognize that the reparations payments of Germany to the Allies were connected with the war debt payments to the United States. This policy of isolation was not exercised when it came to Latin America. At the beginning of the decade the nations south of the Rio Grande were treated as virtual American satellites. Fortunately, this policy was reversed and by the close of the decade better understanding existed.

The kind of international co-operation preferred by the United States in this decade stressed disarmament. The Washington Naval Conference was intended to bolster American policy in the Orient, but led to some reduction in the number of large ships. Other attempts at disarmament were to fail because nations were not prepared to liquidate their arms while still politically insecure. The Kellogg-Briand Pact solemnly denounced war, but added nothing that would ensure peace. The futility of America's foreign policy during the 1920's was fully revealed when the Japanese invaded Manchuria in 1931, and there was no means available to halt such aggression.

Multiple Choice Questions:

______ 1. Which of the following was NOT true of the isolationist policy of the 1920's? 1) High tariffs were passed to keep out foreign goods. 2) Barriers against European immigration were raised. 3) The existence of the League of Nations was ignored. 4) The government remained aloof from all types of international cooperation.

______ 2. The United States refused to recognize the Soviet Union officially because 1) that government had repudiated its debts 2) there was fear of the possible spread of Communism 3) the Soviet Union had challenged America's world leadership 4) other leading nations also refused to recognize the Bolshevik regime.

______ 3. A dispute arose with Mexico in the 1920's over 1) border raids by Mexican bandits 2) attacks on American marines 3) the undue influence of Communists in that country 4) the expropriation of American oil interests.

______ 4. The Washington Naval Conference accomplished all BUT which of the following? 1) A recognition of the Open Door in China. 2) A limitation on land armaments. 3) A limitation on the tonnage of capital ships. 4) Termination of the Anglo-Japanese alliance.

______ 5. Which of the following best describes the Washington Naval Conference in the light of subsequent events? 1) The agreements reached were a needless sacrifice of American interests. 2) It resulted in a betrayal of our policy toward China. 3) The agreements were a spectacular victory for peace in the Pacific. 4) The accords were a worthwhile beginning but were never adequately implemented.

______ 6. The Stimson Doctrine which grew out of the Manchurian crisis was proof that 1) moral ideals without the threat of force carry little weight in international relations 2) the United States was prepared to intervene militarily to enforce its policies 3) the United States warned the League that America had no interest in the Far East 4) the United States was able to check Japanese aggression without the threat of force.

______ 7. The most glaring weakness of the Kellogg-Briand Pact was that 1) the United States failed to sign it 2) very few nations signed it 3) it lacked means to enforce its provisions 4) it was so strong that the United States feared it would drag us into needless wars.

______ 8. America made the collection of war debts more difficult by 1) insisting upon immediate payment 2) charging exorbitant interest rates 3) insisting that war debts and reparations were interwoven 4) raising the tariff so that payment by the European nations was virtually impossible.

_____ **9.** About the best action for the United States in the war debt question would have been 1) a scaling down of the debts 2) forcing Germany to pay higher reparations so that the Allies could afford to pay their war debts 3) canceling the debts with the understanding that the Allies also cancel reparation payments by Germany 4) insisting upon full payment of the money due.

_____ **10.** Attempts at disarmament were doomed to fail in the 1920's because of 1) lack of American participation in the numerous conferences 2) failure to define offensive and defensive weapons 3) the machinations of the munitions makers who sought to scuttle such attempts 4) the deep feeling of insecurity among nations.

Essay Questions:

1. Describe America's attitude toward the Soviet Union in the 1920's. What were the long-range effects of this policy?

2. What led to the calling of the Washington Conference? What did this conference accomplish?

3. Why has the Manchurian crisis of 1931 generally been acknowledged as the first step to World War II? Why was the United States unwilling to make a stand against Japanese policy?

4. Why has the Kellogg-Briand Treaty been described as ably representing the kind of foreign commitment Americans in the 1920's were most interested in?

5. What made the entire war debt problem very difficult to solve? How could this question have been solved?

6. What attempts were made to accomplish disarmament in the 1920's? Why did all of these attempts fail?

Terms, Events, and Personalities to Know:

World Disarmament Conference
Five Power Treaty
Good Neighbor Policy
Dawes Plan
Four Power Treaty
Stimson Doctrine
Young Plan
Manchurian Incident
reparations
Hawley-Smoot Tariff
Nine Power Treaty
Pact of Paris
White Russian

CHAPTER XVIII

A Business Civilization

Summary:

The 1920's were years of dynamic progress and retrogression, of great prosperity and hard times. The majority of people turned from internationalism and reform and concentrated on material things. The economic advance was made possible by the rise of new industries and improvements in sales techniques and financing. While many people made fortunes, labor failed to obtain a fair share of the increase in wealth and the nation's farmers suffered a virtual depression.

With businessmen in political control, the system of regulatory agencies developed during the three preceding administrations was virtually suspended. There was an attempt to return to the extreme laissez-faire economic doctrines current before the Progressive movement. An atmosphere of intolerance made any criticism of American institutions difficult. Political leadership was conspicuous by its absence. Warren G. Harding was perhaps the country's worst President. Calvin Coolidge provided little leadership.

Multiple Choice Questions:

______ **1. Which of the following was NOT descriptive of the 1920's? 1) It was a period of economic growth and progress. 2) Americans tended to reject international commitments. 3) The majority of people seemed content with their lot. 4) There was a broad-based demand for reform in many areas.**

______ **2. Easily outstanding among the new industries of the 1920's was 1) radio 2) movies 3) automobiles 4) aviation.**

______ **3. During the 1920's labor in America 1) enjoyed an increase in real wages 2) became a potent political factor 3) saw an increase in its union strength 4) made appreciable gains as an organized group.**

______ **4. The Republican leadership in the 1920's 1) failed to recognize the economic plight of the farmers 2) virtually suspended the antitrust laws 3) was opposed to governmental regulation 4) stressed a policy of low tariffs.**

______ 5. Oliver Wendell Holmes 1) saw a real danger to American freedom from the subversives 2) believed in complete freedom of speech except when the national security was endangered 3) became the spokesman for the more conservative members of the Supreme Court in civil liberty cases 4) was especially famous for his defense of teachers' loyalty oaths.

______ 6. To judge by the caliber of Harding and Coolidge, the American people in the 1920's wanted 1) dynamic presidential leadership 2) anything but purposeful leadership 3) a continuation of the Progressive movement 4) a continuation of Wilson's policies.

______ 7. The furor raised by the conviction of Sacco and Vanzetti was caused by 1) the general belief that they did not receive a fair trial 2) the fact that Italians supported them 3) the general antagonism of all Americans toward men who held radical beliefs 4) the attempt of Communists to create a popular issue.

______ 8. Perhaps the best explanation as to why Harding received the Republican nomination in 1920 was that 1) his long career of service in the Senate had won him wide support 2) he looked like a President 3) the GOP needed a strong candidate in order to win 4) he resided in a doubtful state.

______ 9. The 1928 election differed most from that of 1924 in that 1) real issues were presented to the voters 2) both candidates were outstanding liberals 3) there was no protest vote 4) the Democratic candidate was weaker.

______ 10. Easily the most competent member of Harding's cabinet was 1) Albert B. Fall 2) Edwin Denby 3) Harry Daugherty 4) Charles E. Hughes.

Essay Questions:

1. Why have the 1920's been described as "one of the most confusing and colorful periods in all American history"?

2. What made possible the astounding growth of the nation's economy in the 1920's?

3. Account for the decline in strength of the labor unions in the decade of the 1920's.

4. Why did the farmers of America fail to share in the prosperity of the 1920's?

5. How did government policy help the revival of laissez-faire doctrines in the 1920's?

6. What characterized the attempt to suppress all criticism in the decade? Why did the nation as a whole condone the widespread subversion of civil liberties?

7. What made the Harding administration one of the most disgraceful in American history?

8. To what extent was Coolidge an improvement over Harding as President?

9. Your text notes that the character of Coolidge was mainly negative. Why, then, should he have enjoyed such tremendous popularity while in the White House?

Terms, Events, and Personalities to Know:

Fordney-McCumber Tariff
Adkins **v** *Children's Hospital*
"tremendous trifles"
Truax **v** *Corrigan*
The Man Nobody Knows
Open Shop
Schenck **v** *United States*
company union
Albert B. Fall
William Green
Abrams **v** *United States*
John W. Davis
Nicola Sacco
Edward L. Doheny
"Ohio gang"
Ku Klux Klan
Charles Evans Hughes
Teapot Dome
Andrew Mellon
Elk Hills
Alfred E. Smith
Harry M. Daugherty

CHAPTER XIX

Social Developments

Summary:

The social changes of the 1920's were to continue those begun before the war. The younger generation rejected the morals and conventions of an older America. The changed relationship between the sexes led to the emancipation of women. The long battle to curb immigration was finally successful. The lawlessness of the decade made enforcement of prohibition difficult and was, in turn, intensified by this effort to legislate against private habits. The revolution in transportation brought the automobile into almost universal use, and the use of the airplane was growing. The radio and the movies helped to standardize American speech and habits without increasing the cultural stature. Spectator sports attracted ever-greater crowds as the result of more leisure time. School enrollment was larger, especially at the high-school level. Newspapers, magazines, and popular novels reached more people than ever before.

Multiple Choice Questions:

_____ 1. The immigration legislation of the 1920's most favored the citizens of 1) Japan 2) Italy 3) Germany 4) England.

_____ 2. The attempt to enforce a national prohibition law led to 1) a rapid expansion of the powers of the federal government 2) a widespread disrespect for law 3) frequent clashes between the powers of state and federal government 4) a virtual split in the Republican party over enforcement.

_____ 3. The most acceptable argument against prohibition was that 1) the Volstead Act was unconstitutional 2) it caused the emergence of gangster elements 3) it was impossible to enforce 4) such a law interfered with individual liberty.

_____ 4. The emancipation of women in the 1920's was accompanied by all of the following EXCEPT 1) a revolution in women's fashions 2) greater stability of the home 3) the influence of Freudianism 4) greater freedoms in the realm of employment.

_____ 5. A basic criticism of the early motion picture industry was that 1) no really good movies were produced 2) the movies lacked popular appeal 3) too many movies gave an unrealistic picture of American life 4) there was no attempt to censor undesirable movies.

_____ 6. The best explanation of the great popularity of spectator sports in the 1920's was 1) the emergence of many outstanding performers 2) the great increase in the amount of leisure time of the average person 3) the building of large stadiums 4) the publicity on the radio for sporting events.

_____ 7. John Dewey was mainly concerned with 1) adjusting the child to his environment 2) bringing the teachings of Freud into the classroom 3) curtailing the elective system 4) retaining an emphasis upon absolute values in the classroom.

_____ 8. One result of larger high-school enrollments was 1) a decline in the cost of education 2) increased emphasis on the college preparatory program 3) an increase in vocational courses 4) a decline in the elective system.

_____ 9. Which of the following did NOT accompany the increasing popularity of radio and the movies? 1) Most programs were tailored to appeal to popular tastes. 2) Advertising exerted a growing influence. 3) There was a sharp decline in the sale of books. 4) Vaudeville became more important.

_____ 10. A very strong argument in favor of the retention of prohibition was that 1) flaunting one law could lead to a breakdown in all law enforcement 2) many churches backed prohibition 3) automobiles and alcohol were incompatible 4) most Americans wanted it.

Essay Questions:

1. Why was the National Origins Act passed? How did this influence immigration into the United States?

2. Why was enforcement of prohibition difficult? Could it have been enforced if the government had had greater interest in enforcement?

3. How did the status of American women change in the 1920's?
4. How did the movies reflect the basic tendencies of the 1920's in America?
5. Why did the importance of spectator sports increase so rapidly in the decade?
6. How did John Dewey influence education in the 1920's?
7. How did the reading habits of the American people reflect the changes taking place in the 1920's?

Terms, Events, and Personalities to Know:

"old immigration"
Model-T
Charles Lindbergh
"new immigration"
Middletown
Volstead Act
Charlie Chaplin
"Scarface Al"
Al Jolson
Twenty-first Amendment
"Big Bill"
Freudianism
Hall-Mills
matriarchy
"monkey trial"

CHAPTER XX

Literature and the Arts Between Wars

Summary:

During the decade of the 1920's there was a strong reaction from the high idealism of the Progressive era and the war period. This reaction was given voice by the so-called "lost"-generation group of writers, who attacked the false values of contemporary society, especially the crass materialism and the emotional and aesthetic starvation. Many of the writers, especially the dramatist Eugene O'Neill, were influenced by the opinions of Freud, who stressed that man should let himself go and not build up frustrations. The criticism of middle-class mores reached a high in the work of Sinclair Lewis, whose books skillfully uncovered the cant, hypocrisy, and false values that were an important part of the American scene.

The writers of the 1930's, in marked contrast to those of the preceding decade, were less obsessed with manners and morals and more concerned with social and economic problems. They were also less critical of the American scene and even tended to find value in American history.

In the period between the wars American music matured. It reached far more people because of the phonograph and the radio. Though the appreciation of classical music was much more extensive, the nation produced few competent composers of serious music. An original contribution of America was the musical form known as jazz. There was much greater appreciation of American artists, sculptors, and architects. By the conclusion of the 1930's Europe had to recognize that the United States had indeed attained cultural independence and in many areas a high level of cultural achievement.

Multiple Choice Questions:

______ **1. In general, the writers of the 1920's 1) continued the traditions of Progressivism 2) extolled the virtues of the business society that was developing 3) were disillusioned with American life 4) advocated a return to the traditions of the nineteenth century.**

______ **2. The high priest of many young intellectuals in the 1920's was 1) John Dos Passos 2) H. L. Mencken 3) Ernest Hemingway 4) Theodore Dreiser.**

______ **3. Those who criticized the social life of America were mainly concerned with 1) emotional and aesthetic starvation 2) clinging to the values of bygone days 3) undue emphasis on religion 4) the impact of the ideas of Darwin on society.**

______ **4. In his dramas Eugene O'Neill was least concerned with 1) Freudian undertones 2) the deep frustration of the human spirit 3) the problems of man's relationship to forces beyond his control 4) showing man's ability to control his own destiny.**

______ **5. Sinclair Lewis' novels 1) stressed blood and violence 2) depicted the plight of the decayed aristocracy of the South 3) vigorously attacked the false values of the business community 4) showed a complete rejection of the American way of life.**

______ **6. Which of the following writers is incorrectly associated? 1) Willa Cather—***Death Comes for the Archbishop* **2) F. Scott Fitzgerald—***The Great Gatsby* **3) T. S. Eliot—***Murder in the Cathedral* **4) William Faulkner—***Desire Under the Elms.*

______ **7. As contrasted with those of the 1920's the writers of the 1930's were more 1) disillusioned 2) concerned with economic and social problems 3) concerned with manners and morals 4) preoccupied with Freudian undertones.**

______ **8. America made an original contribution to music with 1) the operetta 2) the symphony 3) jazz 4) folk music.**

_____ 9. The sculptor responsible for the massive work on Mount Rushmore was 1) Augustus Saint-Gaudens 2) Gutzon Borglum 3) Daniel Chester French 4) Gaston Lachaise.

_____ 10. The paintings of Thomas Hart Benton 1) stressed the degradation and poverty of society 2) were in the tradition of the Ash Can school 3) were usually delicate portraits 4) depicted Midwestern farm scenes.

Essay Questions:

1. Why was pessimism the basic theme in literature during the 1920's? How was it displayed?
2. Compare and contrast the writings of Hemingway and Dos Passos.
3. Why was H. L. Mencken able to become the "high priest" of many intellectuals in the 1920's?
4. What did Sinclair Lewis stress in his writings? Why was Lewis one of the most popular of the critics of American life?
5. What were the recurrent themes to be found in the plays of Eugene O'Neill?
6. How did the literary spirit of the 1930's differ from that of the 1920's?
7. In what ways did Steinbeck and Wolfe typify the writers of the 1930's?
8. To what extent had the culture of the United States been freed of dependence on Europe by the 1930's?

Terms, Events, and Personalities to Know:

Thomas Hart Benton
T. S. Eliot
The Great Gatsby
Thornton Wilder
William Zorach
Mount Rushmore
Maxwell Anderson
Peter Blume
Aaron Copland
Yoknapatawpha
Rodgers and Hammerstein
Stephen Vincent Benet
"proletarian writers"
James T. Farrell
An American Tragedy
Deems Taylor

CHAPTER XXI

Prosperity to Depression

Summary:

Shortly after the inauguration of President Hoover the prosperity of the 1920's came to an abrupt end and the nation faced its most catastrophic depression in history. This economic debacle was caused by the gradual decline of agriculture, certain sick industries, and the unequal distribution of national income, which severely curtailed purchasing power. The spectacular collapse of the stock market signaled the beginning of the depression.

President Hoover attempted to fight the depression by stressing voluntary co-operation by business firms and by restoring public confidence. Once it was obvious that this was not a panic like those of the nineteenth century, President Hoover accepted the new responsibility of government and tried to do something about existing conditions. Unfortunately, the President, who was an outstanding administrator and humanitarian, lacked political experience and was unable to carry out a program effectively. He suggested many steps which might have aided the nation's economy, but he usually was too slow in his efforts to carry them out.

In the 1932 campaign President Hoover appeared to the nation to be indifferent to the problems created by the depression. The Democratic nominee, Franklin Delano Roosevelt, promised action and stressed during his campaign that the federal government had a direct obligation for the health of the nation's economy.

Multiple Choice Questions:

______ **1. One important cause of the depression was 1) the draining of gold abroad 2) the fact that agriculture took too large a share of the national income 3) an unequal distribution of the national income 4) governmental interference with banking.**

______ **2. President Hoover first attempted to meet the problem of the depression by 1) direct federal relief 2) volunteer measures and by restoring confidence 3) a program of public works 4) loaning money to business.**

_____ 3. President Hoover's most significant weakness lay in the fact that he 1) lacked administrative experience 2) lacked a social conscience 3) was not ready to break with precedent and lend government assistance in the emergency 4) lacked political aptitude.

_____ 4. The Hoover administration was most vigorously criticized for its 1) false optimism concerning business conditions 2) failure to intervene more energetically to aid business 3) farm policies 4) handling of the bonus marchers.

_____ 5. The basic weakness of the Agricultural Marketing Act was 1) its efforts to control too many crops 2) the failure to provide enough funds to handle the program 3) the failure to limit production 4) the failure to provide for storage facilities.

_____ 6. The Hawley-Smoot Tariff of 1930 1) was one of Hoover's most constructive depression measures 2) effectively lowered tariff rates 3) accentuated the forces making for world-wide depression 4) aided the farm program.

_____ 7. The Reconstruction Finance Corporation 1) loaned money to banks and big businesses 2) created work projects for the unemployed 3) loaned money for direct relief purposes 4) expanded public works.

_____ 8. Roosevelt's campaign in 1932 differed from that of Hoover in that Roosevelt stressed 1) economy in government 2) spelling out his exact program of relief 3) retaining prohibition 4) using the government to safeguard the economic interests of all classes.

_____ 9. NOT a cause of the depression was 1) the decline in agriculture 2) the existence of many sick industries 3) too much money being used for speculative purposes 4) the bankruptcy of the federal government.

_____ 10. About the only thing definite about the election of 1932 is that 1) the country was on the threshold of revolution 2) Hoover was able to stir much popular enthusiasm by his campaign 3) Roosevelt won because he was able to spell out his program 4) practically any Democratic candidate could have won.

Essay Questions:

1. Discuss the causes of the depression.

2. How was President Hoover well qualified for the presidency? Why did Hoover have so much difficulty as President?

3. How did Hoover attempt to solve the problems created by the depression? To what extent did his personal political philosophy hamper his efforts to meet the emergency with which he was confronted?

4. Why was Hoover's farm program doomed to failure?

5. To what extent was Hoover justified in claiming that his administration began "the most gigantic program of economic defense and counterattack ever evolved in the history of the Republic"?

6. How did Roosevelt's campaign of 1932 differ from other presidential campaigns? Why were the election results foreordained?

7. With severe economic conditions, why was there no threat of an uprising of the people against the government in the depth of the depression?

Terms, Events, and Personalities to Know:

Commonwealth Club speech	**Agricultural Marketing Act**
Bonus Expeditionary Force	**"Black Thursday"**
McNary-Haugen Bill	**Muscle Shoals**
"trickle-down theory"	**John J. Raskob**
Great Engineer	**Hoovervilles**

CHAPTER XXII

Advent of the New Deal

Summary:

Although considered by many to be a radical, Franklin Delano Roosevelt was actually a conservative. A member of a prominent family of New York aristocrats, he had never been associated with ideas which could be defined as even mildly radical. His first act as President was to try to restore the confidence of the American people in themselves, a task at which President Hoover had failed. Essentially, Roosevelt wanted to enact a program similar to that of the Progressive era. He desired to preserve but regulate capitalism in America. A charming individual and proven politician, the first to recognize the value of radio to the chief executive, he was able to present his program in a favorable light to the nation.

Roosevelt promptly called on Congress during the famous one hundred days to enact a series of important relief measures. In addition to the Emergency Relief Acts, the banks were placed on a firmer footing. The relief program enacted by the Democrats was most extensive and most expensive. Whenever possible it stressed work programs such as the Works Progress Administration instead of the direct dole. A relief program for farmers provided for the payment of subsidies on certain farm products to those farmers who agreed to limit production of these products and thus put an end to farm surpluses. One of the least successful parts of the Roosevelt program was the National Recovery Act, a measure wherein business was supposed to eliminate unfair competition. Instead, this measure fostered monopoly and actually hurt small businesses. Once the immediate crisis was met, the New Deal attempted to put into effect a recovery program. The plans included the devaluation of the dollar, an expanded public works program, and a more extensive control of agriculture. In spite of these measures the nation's economy did not make substantial improvements after the first two years of the New Deal.

Multiple Choice Questions:

_____ **1. Which of the following statements is NOT applicable to President Franklin D. Roosevelt? 1) He was a militant reformer with a carefully planned program. 2) He was an able politician. 3) His radiant personality enabled him to attract much popular support. 4) He approached the powers of the presidency in much the same way as did Theodore Roosevelt.**

_____ **2. Franklin D. Roosevelt was 1) a profound thinker 2) thoroughly conversant with the economic problems of the day 3) aloof and reserved 4) a poor admininstrator.**

_____ **3. The basic objective of Franklin D. Roosevelt was to 1) start the nation on the road to socialism 2) reform but preserve capitalism 3) continue the policies of the 1920's 4) institute his own economic system.**

_____ **4. The New Deal acted first to 1) save big business firms on the brink of bankruptcy 2) create massive relief programs 3) restore confidence in the banks 4) relieve agricultural distress.**

_____ **5. As contrasted with President Hoover, Roosevelt was 1) prepared to use the federal government in an effort to solve the depression 2) not greatly concerned about the legality of his actions 3) reluctant to expand the powers of the federal government to meet the emergency 4) more interested in economy in government.**

_____ **6. A New Deal agency which aided the cause of conservation was the 1) NYA 2) CCC 3) PWA 4) TNEC.**

_____ **7. The relief program of the Works Progress Administration was intended to 1) provide direct relief aid to the needy 2) arrange make-work projects in manual labor only 3) aid the morale of many different types of workers 4) reach only a few workers.**

_____ 8. Roosevelt's devaluation of the dollar 1) vastly increased national purchasing power 2) had no important effect on the national economy 3) led to the printing of greenbacks 4) caused a prompt rise in commodity prices.

_____ 9. The second AAA emphasized 1) conservation 2) aid to the small farmer 3) the first limitation upon crop production 4) a tax on food processors for its financing.

_____ 10. A just criticism of the NRA was that it 1) discriminated against labor 2) was not extensive enough in character 3) tended to foster monopoly 4) tended to foster too much competition.

Essay Questions:

1. What were FDR's greatest assets as the nation's leader in a time of crisis? What were his weaknesses?
2. How did Roosevelt view the powers of the presidency?
3. Describe the basic features of the hundred days.
4. How did the New Deal approach the problem of relief in America? What was distinctive about this relief program? Upon what grounds could it be criticized?
5. What steps did the New Deal take to relieve the distress of the farmer? To what extent was its agricultural program successful?
6. What was the NRA? Why was it inconsistent with many features of the New Deal?

Terms, Events, and Personalities to Know:

"sick chicken case"
London Economic Conference
NYA
Hugh Johnson
PWA
"an ever-normal granary"
CWA
TVA
parity
WPA
marginal land
devaluation
Harry Hopkins
tariff reciprocity
FERA
CCC
Emergency Banking Act
Harold Ickes
SEC

CHAPTER XXIII

Reform and Social Security

Summary:

The New Deal stressed basic reform after 1935. President Roosevelt believed that basic inequities existed within the nation and that only by creating an atmosphere of more extensive economic opportunity would the nation be on the road to prosperity. To accomplish this the relief agencies such as WPA and PWA were utilized. In his economic bill of rights the President stressed that the function of government was no longer just to protect political rights but now included the duty of protecting economic rights as well.

The Tennessee Valley Authority was one of the more significant long-range undertakings of the New Deal. It was actually compounded of recovery, relief, and reform. The plan was to overhaul completely an entire area of the country by producing cheap electricity to encourage industry, by flood control and irrigation for agricultural purposes, and by providing recreational facilities. The Social Security Act tried to meet the problem of what workmen would do when they were unemployed. Of more importance, it attempted to establish a system of retirement that would take many old people off the labor market. The New Deal acted to assist labor out of genuine humanitarian impulses and also out of political necessity. President Roosevelt encouraged the workers to organize and helped them obtain certain minimal standards.

In spite of all of the measures enacted by the New Deal, economic recovery did not actually take place until the advent of World War II. Federal agencies became more numerous, with comparable growth in the cost of the government. However, the New Deal had established a new economic constitutional order which intervened directly and indirectly in every phase of the country's economic activity. This has continued to the present day.

Multiple Choice Questions:

______ 1. The part of the TVA program that became most controversial concerned 1) flood control 2) the production of electricity 3) the prevention of erosion 4) reforestation.

______ 2. Which of the following was NOT true of the Social Security Act of 1935? 1) It was enthusiastically supported by President Roosevelt. 2) It provided for retirement pay. 3) The United States was the first nation to enact such legislation. 4) A system of unemployment compensation was provided.

______ 3. The Wagner Act was 1) a part of Roosevelt's original program 2) the most popular New Deal measure 3) vigorously resisted by the business community 4) opposed by organized labor.

______ 4. One failing of the original Social Security Act was that it 1) set the tax rate too high for the workers 2) was improperly administered 3) lacked the support of the general public 4) did not include many types of workers.

______ 5. The WPA 1) prepared the way for the TVA program 2) helped preserve the talents of many artists 3) stressed a straight dole 4) was most effective in assuring permanent rehabilitation.

______ 6. In his "Economic Bill of Rights" Roosevelt was most interested in 1) creating the welfare state 2) infuriating the Republicans 3) earning the political backing of the lower classes 4) safeguarding the economic rights of all the people.

______ 7. The Fair Labor Standards Act provided for all of the following EXCEPT 1) a guarantee that labor would be free to organize into unions 2) a minimum wage 3) banning child labor 4) a maximum work week.

Essay Questions:

1. How did the WPA have a significant cultural impact upon the nation?

2. What were the purposes of the TVA? To what extent did it accomplish these purposes? Why was it so vigorously criticized?

3. What were the aims of the Social Security Act? Was such legislation really needed? Why was this program universally supported?

4. Why did the New Deal tend to veer more toward the left after 1935?

5. How was the New Deal approach to the rights of labor revolutionary? What were the provisions of the Wagner Act and the Fair Labor Standards Act?

6. How did the New Deal influence the coming of a new economic order?

Terms, Events, and Personalities to Know:

Holding Company Act
Wagner Act
Economic Bill of Rights
National Labor Relations Act

"yardstick"
"cease and desist"
David E. Lilienthal
Norris-La Guardia Act

CHAPTER XXIV

The Rise of Labor

Summary:

One significant result of the New Deal was the rise to prominence of organized labor. Since shortly after the Civil War labor had struggled for national recognition only to find public opinion and most of the agencies of the federal government aligned against it. Under the Democrats in the 1930's the organization of labor unions was not only tolerated but was actually encouraged. This growth of unions was not to be accomplished without controversy, even within the ranks of labor itself. The A. F. of L. was opposed to industrial unionism and desired to continue its practice of protecting the more experienced craftsman and of ignoring the less skilled workman. John L. Lewis, the head of the United Mine Workers, believed that the future of organized labor rested on the organization of the mass-production industries and especially of the unskilled workman. As a result of this difference Lewis led his following out of the A. F. of L. and organized the C. I. O.

Through its strenuous organizing activity, the C. I. O. was soon able to have effective unions in the steel, automobile, rubber, and textile industries. As these constituted the bulk of the large mass-production industries, the goals of the union could be said to have been realized. With this emergence of big labor, it was inevitable that it be involved in political activity. In the 1936 election labor, in general, gave its support to the New Deal, which had befriended it. As organized labor grew in size and power, it sometimes did not act in the public interest. In fact it was as guilty of misusing its power as industry had been. This caused a public reaction against organized labor, a reaction which became stronger during the early years of World War II.

Multiple Choice Questions:

_____ 1. The most important explanation of the growth in strength of organized labor during the New Deal was 1) the militancy of labor organizers 2) the rising prosperity 3) the encouragement of the government 4) the fact that business was now ready to accept labor.

_____ 2. The A. F. of L. was 1) most interested in organizing workers in the mass-production industries 2) most interested in craft unionism 3) characterized by dynamic leadership in the 1930's 4) devoid of controversy during the 1930's.

_____ 3. Easily the most dynamic leader of organized labor in the 1930's was 1) Philip Murray 2) William Green 3) Sidney Hillman 4) John L. Lewis.

_____ 4. The "Memorial Day Massacre" resulted from labor's attempt to organize 1) the automotive industry 2) Southern textiles 3) the steel industry 4) agricultural workers.

_____ 5. The attempt to organize the automobile industry 1) was marked by much violence 2) saw the Michigan governor intervene to aid the employers 3) saw the mass use of picketing 4) was characterized by the first use of the sit-down strike.

_____ 6. As contrasted with the A. F. of L., the C.I.O. was mainly interested in 1) organizing craft unions 2) organizing the workmen in the mass-production industries 3) organizing the automobile workers 4) keeping nonwhites out of their unions.

_____ 7. When it came to political activity the C.I.O. 1) ignored all political activity 2) usually supported the New Deal 3) attempted to organize a separate party 4) openly espoused the Communist cause.

_____ 8. Which of the following did NOT characterize the labor movement of the 1930's? 1) Jurisdictional disputes between rival unions 2) Some instances of labor racketeering. 3) The responsible leadership of John L. Lewis. 4) Nationwide strikes that could paralyze the nation's economy.

_____ 9. The C.I.O. first was able to organize 1) steel 2) rubber 3) coal 4) textiles.

_____ 10. The growth of organized labor in the 1930's was marked by 1) the widespread infiltration of labor by Communists 2) greater responsibility on the part of union leaders 3) the passage of much antilabor legislation 4) the growing political power of labor.

Essay Questions:

1. Account for the rapid expansion of organized labor in the 1930's.
2. What was the source of John L. Lewis' differences with the A. F. of L.?
3. Why was the C.I.O. able to organize the automobile workers?
4. How did the unions participate in politics in the 1930's?
5. Why was there a reaction against organized labor in the late 1930's?

Terms, Events, and Personalities to Know:

- **Philip Murray**
- **"Little Steel"**
- **American Labor Party**
- **"Big Steel"**
- **Non-Partisan League**
- **Political Action League**
- **"Memorial Day Massacre"**
- **industrial unionism**
- **"sit-downs"**

CHAPTER XXV

Close of a Decade

Summary:

When President Roosevelt first took office in the midst of the crisis in March 1933, he had the support of virtually everyone in the nation. This honeymoon was short-lived, and by 1934 much opposition had developed to his policies. Many people were alienated by the cost of the New Deal and by the introduction of what they considered to be revolutionary measures. Some two-thirds of the nation's newspapers were consistently opposed to the policies of President Roosevelt. In spite of this the Democrats increased their margin in Congress in 1934. In the election of 1936 the Republicans attacked the New Deal with all the resources available to them. Their candidate was Governor Landon of Kansas, an able individual but one who lacked national prominence. Amid charges of demagoguery, dictatorship, and even communism against the New Deal, it was obvious that a new kind of election was in the making. For the first time politics were divided strictly along class lines with the lower classes voting overwhelmingly for the Democrats and the Republicans attracting the suport of the wealthy. It was inevitable that the G.O.P. should lose.

After the election F.D.R. attacked the Supreme Court, believing that it had attempted to curtail his program. Perhaps as a result of the attack on the judiciary, the court changed its mind on several key measures, and Roosevelt's attempt to reorganize the judiciary was defeated.

In the Congressional election of 1938 President Roosevelt suffered another political reverse.

With the passage of years the New Deal, one of the nation's most controversial administrations, can be more fairly evaluated. On the negative side it failed to bring about complete economic recovery. It brought big government with the attendant evils of bureaucracy. On the positive side, it revived faith in democratic capitalism and helped alter the nation's economy so that more people shared in the wealth that was produced. Though the New Deal was admittedly expensive, it can be argued that the conservation of natural resources that it effected may have offset the cost by increasing the physical wealth of the nation.

Multiple Choice Questions:

______ **1. A just criticism of the New Deal is that 1) Congressional powers were usurped by the Chief Executive 2) it was very expensive 3) there was no effort to solve the nation's problems 4) business conditions failed to improve under it.**

______ **2. 1) Huey Long 2) The Rev. Charles E. Coughlin 3) Francis E. Townsend 4) Harry Hopkins was a consistent supporter of New Deal policies.**

______ **3. In 1936 the Republican standard bearer 1) made a better showing than had Hoover in 1932 2) was an Eastern conservative 3) carried only two states 4) had a dynamic personality.**

______ **4. President Roosevelt attempted to handle the opposition of the Supreme Court by 1) recalling the justices opposed to his program 2) adding a justice for each justice over seventy years of age 3) ending the right of judicial review 4) winning the support of Chief Justice Hughes.**

______ **5. In his conflict with the judiciary Roosevelt 1) suffered a complete defeat 2) was able to get his legislative program through Congress with some amendments 3) was able to obtain much Republican support 4) may have lost a battle but ended by winning the war.**

______ **6. Which of the following members of Roosevelt's official family failed to support the President consistently? 1) Henry Wallace 2) James Farley 3) Cordell Hull 4) Harold Ickes.**

______ **7. The elections of what year could be considered a set-back for President Roosevelt? 1) 1932 2) 1934 3) 1936 4) 1938.**

______ **8. With the passage of years the New Deal has come to be recognized 1) for having completely solved the problems of the depression 2) as a series of ill-fated socialistic experiments 3) as a serious attempt to revive faith in democratic capitalism 4) as an experiment which lost a great deal of the taxpayer's money.**

_____ 9. As President, Franklin D. Roosevelt 1) tended to be usually indecisive 2) was undisputed leader of his party and the country 3) lacked personality and charm 4) always displayed a firm grasp of the nation's economic issues.

_____ 10. The election of 1936 was different from most presidential contests because it was fought on 1) the NRA 2) the tariff 3) class lines 4) religion.

Essay Questions:

1. What was the primary basis of the New Deal political support?
2. What elements in America opposed the New Deal from the Right? What elements opposed it from the Left?
3. How did the election of 1936 differ from previous presidential contests? How decisive were the results?
4. What prompted the dispute between F.D.R. and the Supreme Court? How did Roosevelt plan to reorganize the Supreme Court?
5. Why did Roosevelt's challenge of the judiciary provoke so much controversy? To what extent did F.D.R., in the long run, win the contest with the Court?
6. Evaluate the kind of talent that Roosevelt surrounded himself with. How was he able to control his party?
7. Account for the political reverses suffered by the New Deal in the 1938 election.
8. How was the New Deal a blessing to America? How did its policies work against the best interests of the country?

Terms, Events, and Personalities to Know:

Rexford G. Tugwell
Steward Machine Company v *Davis*
Harry Hopkins
National Labor Relations Board v *Jones and Laughlin*
Henry Wallace
fireside chat
Frances Perkins
Alfred M. Landon
Hugo Black
Liberty League
James A. Farley
Upton Sinclair
Raymond Moley
"Louisiana Kingfish"
Rev. Charles E. Coughlin
United States v *Butler*
William Lemke

CHAPTER XXVI

Neutrality

Summary:

During his first administration President Roosevelt was so preoccupied with domestic affairs that the international scene received little attention. This was in accord with the attitude of the American public. Most Americans were disillusioned as a result of World War I and believed that they could remain indifferent to the outcome of another war. After trouble began in Europe, Congress passed a series of neutrality laws intended to keep the nation from repeating the steps which presumably took us into World War I. By the fall of 1937 President Roosevelt was beginning to realize that isolationism was not a wise policy, and he expressed this in his speech calling for a quarantine of aggressors. However, without the support of the nation he was powerless to act.

When war broke out in the fall of 1939 most Americans were stunned at what had happened, but were firmly convinced that it was none of our business. President Roosevelt obtained the repeal of much of the neutrality legislation by arguing that these laws aided the dictators who had already prepared for war and harmed countries that were prevented from buying from the United States after war had started. It was not until the fall of France in June 1940 that Americans realized that Hitler was a threat to them.

Multiple Choice Questions:

______ **1. American isolation of the 1920's and 1930's grew out of 1) fear of the military might of Hitler 2) the belief of many Americans that Asia was more important to the United States than Europe 3) the deliberate attempt of the nation's leadership to avoid all foreign commitments 4) popular disillusionment with the results of World War I.**

______ **2. The Stimson Doctrine 1) was a reinterpretation of the Monroe Doctrine 2) committed the United States not to recognize territorial changes obtained by force 3) denied the United States the right to intervene in Latin America 4) offered the protection of the United States to all of the Western Hemisphere.**

_____ 3. The neurality laws of the 1930's rested on the assumption that 1) Hitler would easily win Europe 2) England and France were capable of defending themselves 3) the United States could remain indifferent to the results of a general war 4) the United States would have to aid the democracies of the world.

_____ 4. The Ludlow Referendum 1) would have given the President greater freedom of action in times of crisis 2) implied much confidence in the Constitution as originally written 3) would have given Congress the authority to declare war 4) implied that only the people could judge when it is proper for a democracy to wage war.

_____ 5. Between 1937 and the outbreak of the war in 1939 1) most Americans remained complacent 2) Congress repealed the neutrality laws because they aided the aggressors 3) President Roosevelt tried to arouse the American people to the dangers inherent in a general war 4) President Roosevelt actively supported English policy against Hitler.

_____ 6. Once the European war began most Americans 1) favored the Allies but still wanted to remain neutral 2) wanted to enter the war on the side of the Allies 3) favored Germany and Italy 4) had no opinion on the war.

_____ 7. The American people most bitterly resented Russia's attack on 1) Poland 2) Romania 3) Finland 4) Estonia.

_____ 8. The event that finally convinced the American people that some defense against possible aggression was necessary was 1) Germany's attack upon Russia 2) the fall of France 3) Pearl Harbor 4) Germany's conquest of Norway.

_____ 9. When President Roosevelt referred to "the hand that held the dagger" he was referring to 1) Japan's attack on Pearl Harbor 2) Russia's attack on Poland 3) Germany's invasion of Holland and Belgium 4) Italy's entry into World War II.

_____ 10. The outbreak of World War II in Europe became inevitable after 1) the Munich Pact 2) France surrendered 3) the United States refused to repeal its neutrality legislation 4) Germany and Russia signed a nonaggression pact.

Essay Questions:

1. What was the attitude of the American people toward foreign affairs in the 1930's? What caused this attitude?

2. Outline the provisions of the neutrality legislation of the 1930's. What was the purpose of this legislation?

3. How did Roosevelt attempt to alter neutrality legislation (1937–39)? Why were so many people opposed to F.D.R.'s foreign policy?

4. Trace the events in Europe from Munich to December 1941. Why did the United States have so little influence on European affairs?

5. How did the fall of France influence American policy and American public opinion?

6. Would a retention of the neutrality laws have kept America out of the war?

Terms, Events, and Personalities to Know:

"rape of Finland"
"phony war"
"quarantine speech"
Ludlow Referendum
Munich Conference
Good Neighbor Policy
"merchants of death"
Non-Intervention Committee
cash and carry program

CHAPTER XXVII

Pearl Harbor

Summary:

During the summer of 1940 President Roosevelt stressed a policy of aiding England by all measures short of war. Arms and munitions were furnished to the British. Meanwhile, the nation took a series of steps to prepare itself in the event of war, even going so far as to institute a peacetime military draft. Many people vigorously opposed Roosevelt's policies and argued that we should be completely neutral and ignore what happened to the British. The debates between the interventionists and the isolationists became most acrimonious and frequently crossed party lines. The public opinion polls showed the indecision of the American people. Most people wanted England to win, but also wanted the United States to remain neutral.

The election of 1940 found Roosevelt taking the unprecedented step of running for a third term against Wendell Willkie, a competent Republican adversary. Reluctance to change administrations with the threat of war before the nation doubtless aided Roosevelt in his precedent-shattering bid for a third term. Once the election was over, the administration passed the Lend-Lease Act to assist the British. This led to an undeclared war in the Atlantic, with German submarines attacking American ships.

With neither the American people nor the government able to decide about the European war, the matter was settled for them in the

Pacific by the Japanese. The long-standing disagreement between Japan and the United States had its origins in the efforts of the Americans to enforce the Open Door Policy. Since the days of Theodore Roosevelt American foreign policy had defended China, especially against the designs of an expansionist Japan. From 1931 on, the Japanese became more aggressive toward China, and they launched an all-out assault in 1937. The United States could have had peace with Japan at any time simply by approving Japan's plans to annex China. This the administration was not prepared to do. After many years of fruitless negotiations Japan attacked the American fleet at Pearl Harbor. Japan's alliance with Germany and Italy prompted those nations to declare war on the United States, and our position in the European war was finally settled.

Multiple Choice Questions:

_____ **1. In order to win bipartisan support for his preparedness program Roosevelt appointed a Republican to his cabinet in 1940 named 1) Alfred Landon 2) Henry Stimson 3) Wendell Willkie 4) Charles McNary.**

_____ **2. The most important move to aid the British in 1940 was 1) the passage of lend-lease 2) the use of American warships to protect the British Isles 3) the destroyer-naval base deal 4) the loaning of money to the British for purchases in the United States.**

_____ **3. In the election of 1940 1) the Republicans suffered another catastrophic defeat 2) Roosevelt won but the Democrats failed to carry Congress 3) the Republican candidate lacked any real popular following 4) a tradition started by Washington was broken.**

_____ **4. The basic difference between the United States and Japan in the Far East grew out of 1) Japan's desire to control China 2) an American embargo on war materiel to Japan 3) Japanese designs on the Dutch East Indies 4) Japanese designs upon the Philippines.**

_____ **5. The Congressional vote for war against Japan was 1) comparable to that which began World War I 2) unanimous 3) by the Democrats mainly 4) with only a single dissenting vote.**

_____ **6. The best explanation for the success of the Japanese sneak attack upon Pearl Harbor is that 1) there was a conspiracy in Washington to get the United States into war 2) American military authorities were as complacent as was the general public 3) Washington believed the attack would hit the Philippines first 4) Japanese intelligence deliberately misled the Americans.**

_____ **7. The Japanese attack upon Pearl Harbor was unique in history because 1) it had been prepared years in advance 2) it was carried on with the backing of Germany 3) peaceful diplomatic negotiations were still in progress 4) the entire American Pacific fleet was destroyed in a single battle.**

______ 8. Men of such diverse backgrounds as John L. Lewis, Senator Wheeler, and former President Hoover were joined together 1) in their support of the administration's foreign policy, 1939–41 2) in that they were all members of the same political party 3) in that they were all opposed to the administration's foreign policy, 1939–41 4) in that they were all members of the Committee to Aid the Allies.

______ 9. By the fall of 1941 1) the United States Navy was fighting an undeclared war in the Atlantic 2) most Americans were expecting the Japanese attack 3) Roosevelt had secretly promised Churchill that the United States would enter the war 4) the United States was sending military equipment to England, but had refused all aid to Russia.

______ 10. Which is the correct chronological order of the following events of 1941? A) The attack upon Pearl Harbor B) Passage of the Lend-Lease Bill C) Announcement of the Atlantic Charter D) Germany and Italy declared war on the United States. 1) D,C,B,A 2) B,C,A,D 3) C,A,D,B 4) A,D,B,C.

Essay Questions:

1. What was the position of the isolationists in the year before the war? What was the position of the interventionists?
2. What steps did President Roosevelt take to prepare the nation for war between the time of the fall of France and Pearl Harbor? Upon what basis could these steps be criticized?
3. Discuss the basic issues of the 1940 campaign. Why was Roosevelt able to win?
4. What were the Lend-Lease Act and the Atlantic Charter? Why were they steps away from neutrality?
5. Upon what basis might Hitler have protested America's breach of neutrality?
6. Describe the basis of the dispute between the United States and Japan in the Orient. How could this dispute have been settled without war?
7. How did the administration attempt to restrain Japan? Why were these efforts a failure?
8. It has been frequently claimed that F.D.R. tricked the Japanese into attacking Pearl Harbor. What has been the basis of such claims? How valid are they?

Terms, Events, and Personalities to Know:

Henry L. Stimson
Committee to Defend America
Wendell L. Willkie
Frank Knox
"Reuben James"
Cordell Hull
William S. Knudsen
"give us the tools"
Selective Service
Axis powers
Act of Havana
"Greer"
destroyer-naval base deal

CHAPTER XXVIII

Total War

Summary:

The division of opinion over foreign policy within the United States was ended by the Japanese attack on Pearl Harbor. From this time on, the American people were united on a single goal—victory. The major decisions of the war were made by President Roosevelt, who decided that Hitler was the chief enemy and was to be defeated first. In World War II the total mobilization of the home front was on a scale that completely dwarfed that of World War I. All of industry was brought under government control, and science was used to develop many new weapons, including the atom bomb. The control of labor, prices, and costs was not left to voluntary restriction as in the earlier war, but this time controls were complete and relatively tight. A fortunate difference from World War I was the almost total lack of flamboyant patriotism and war hysteria. During World War II most Americans were simply interested in getting the war over as quickly as possible.

When the United States entered the war Hitler had just completed a long series of victories, and there was some fear that our allies could not hold out until America had developed a war machine. A basic difference between American and British policy arose over the question of a second front. The British did not want to attack in France, but preferred to attack in southern Europe. The Americans wanted to hit the Germans as quickly as possible near their nerve center. A compromise was evolved wherein the initial invasion of the Americans was in North Africa, and then in Italy. The cross Channel invasion did not materialize until June 1944. The war in Europe ended in May 1945 with the assistance of the Russian army, which was largely equipped with American supplies.

On the Pacific front the Japanese were everywhere victorious for almost the first year of the war. They were first checked at Guadalcanal in the fall of 1942. From this time on, the Americans seized a number of islands as bases from which their ships and planes could operate. After Germany was defeated all of the resources of the allies were concentrated against Japan, which, with the aid of the atom bomb, was defeated in August 1945. President Roosevelt, the chief architect of the victory, who had been re-elected in 1944, died in April 1945.

Multiple Choice *Questions:*

_____ 1. In what respect did the Japanese attack on Pearl Harbor aid the American war effort? 1) The Japanese losses reduced that nation's offensive potential. 2) It made the Orient the number one objective of the American war effort. 3) It enabled the nation to enter the war unified as to purpose. 4) It destroyed mostly obsolete naval vessels.

_____ 2. During World War II the number of Americans entering the military forces was 1) five million 2) ten million 3) fifteen million 4) twenty million.

_____ 3. As contrasted with World War I, the efforts to control inflation during World War II 1) stressed an appeal to voluntary co-operation of the general public 2) were stricter and far more effective 3) halted all inflation 4) were free from public criticism.

_____ 4. A distinct improvement on the home front during World War II was 1) the relative absence of flamboyant patriotism 2) the absence of profiteering 3) the absence of governmental regulations 4) the complete absence of labor strife.

_____ 5. The first check to the calamitous string of Japanese victories came in the 1) Battle of Midway 2) Battle of Guadalcanal 3) Battle of Kasserine Pass 4) Battle of the Coral Sea.

_____ 6. The most significant difference between the United States and Britain on how the war should be fought was over 1) the amount of aid that should be given to Russia 2) the surrender terms offered to the Axis 3) a cross Channel invasion 4) negotiations with Vichy France.

_____ 7. Of these battles of World War II, A) Pearl Harbor B) the Bulge C) North Africa D) Iwo Jima, which of the following arrangements is chronologically correct? 1) D,B,A,C 2) A,B,C,D 3) D,A,B,C 4) A,C,B,D.

_____ 8. The election of 1944 can be interpreted as an indication that 1) Roosevelt had lost his vote-getting ability 2) the nation was prepared to repudiate "the tired old men" 3) America was prepared to accept responsibility for postwar co-operation 4) the third-term issue was still important.

_____ 9. In his decision to drop the atomic bomb President Truman acted 1) because he wanted to end the war before the Russians could enter 2) because he believed that countless American lives would be saved 3) in order to punish Japan for having started the war 4) in order to end the kamikaze raids.

_____ 10. Early in the war President Roosevelt decided that American strategy should call for 1) the defeat of Japan first 2) the defeat of Hitler first 3) an immediate cross Channel invasion 4) ignoring the German submarines as they could sink few allied ships.

Essay Questions:

1. To what extent was the Japanese attack upon Pearl Harbor one of the biggest blunders of the war?

2. Why did Roosevelt do an outstanding job as the nation's war leader?

3. What were the reasons why Germany instead of Japan was selected as the primary enemy?

4. What were the basic differences between the British and American leaders on the conduct of the war?

5. How was America's productive capacity harnessed for war? How effective as a weapon of war was American industry?

6. Compare and contrast the controls of the economy and the regulation of the home front during World War II with those during World War I.

7. "Neither the flamboyant patriotism nor the hysteria of the war years a quarter century earlier were very much in evidence." Account for this change in attitude during World War II.

8. Trace the main events in the War of the Pacific. Why was it very difficult to carry on the war in this theater?

9. Trace the events in the European theater. What were the pivotal points that spelled victory for the Allies?

10. Did the Allies make a mistake by delaying a second front until 1944? Could the war have been ended earlier if the invasion had taken place in 1943?

Terms, Events, and Personalities to Know:

"Repulse"
Battle of the Atlantic
"island-hopping"
Operation Overland
Battle of the Coral Sea
"tired old men"
"Hump"
Battle of Midway
Donald Nelson
Battle of Leyte Gulf
"Manhattan District"
Guadalcanal
War Labor Disputes Act
Operation Torch
Teheran
OPA
Kasserine Pass
Dumbarton Oaks
Battle of Stalingrad
kamikaze
Iwo Jima

Map Exercise III

Locate the following:

1. **London**
2. **Normandy**
3. **The Rhine**
4. **The Elbe**
5. **Berlin**
6. **Anzio**
7. **Sicily**
8. **Stalingrad**
9. **Casablanca**
10. **Yalta**

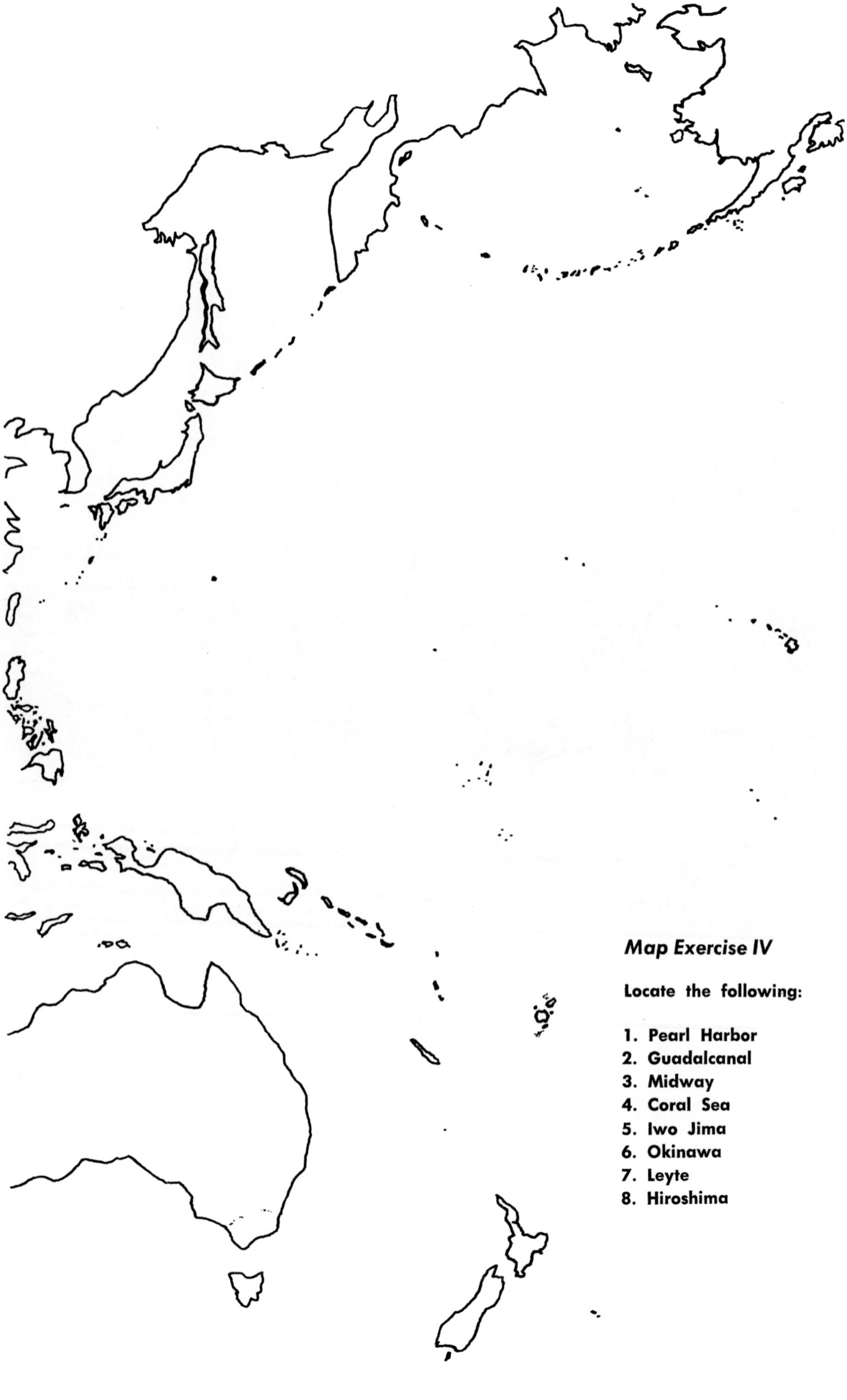

Map Exercise IV

Locate the following:

1. **Pearl Harbor**
2. **Guadalcanal**
3. **Midway**
4. **Coral Sea**
5. **Iwo Jima**
6. **Okinawa**
7. **Leyte**
8. **Hiroshima**

CHAPTER XXIX

The Postwar Scene

Summary:

The periods immediately following wars in American history have always been marked by confusion, uncertainty, and unrest. The period following World War II was especially difficult because of the nature of total war. Among the problems that needed solution were the demobilization of the army, the disposal of the properties owned by the government, the end of price control, the reorganization of the government, and the solution of the problems created by the development of atomic energy. It was difficult to adjust these problems because of the lack of co-operation between the new President and Congress. The situation was made more difficult after the elections of 1946, when the Republicans were returned to power for the first time since 1932.

In spite of all the problems that had to be met after the war, the readjustment proceeded more smoothly than had been anticipated. Veterans were quickly assimilated into peacetime activity, largely because of the tremendous expansion of industrial production. Labor tried to preserve or extend the gains that it had made during the 1930's and during the war. Many employers felt that the time was opportune for the reduction of the strength of organized labor. As a result the nation was swept by a series of strikes. The growing antagonism toward labor resulted in the passage by Congress of the Taft-Hartley Law, which was intended to redress a balance in industrial relations in favor of the employers.

When Harry S. Truman became President after Roosevelt's death in 1945 very little was known of him. His selection as Vice-President had been almost accidental. During the immediate postwar years his numerous difficulties with Congress caused many to be skeptical of his abilities. Most Republicans were certain that he would be defeated in the 1948 election. Even the Democrats did not want him as their standard bearer. The Southerners put up their own candidate because President Truman had favored a program of civil rights. Henry Wallace led many liberals out of the Democratic party into a group called the Progressive party. No election had been so completely decided before the votes were counted as that of 1948. Everyone assumed that Dewey, the Republican nominee, would be elected. When the results were in, the greatest upset in political history had occurred and Truman had been elected to the presidency in his own right.

Multiple Choice Questions:

_____ **1.** **As contrasted to the period following World War I, the post-World War II period in the United States was characterized by all BUT which of the following? 1) Quick demobilization of the military forces. 2) A Red scare. 3) Labor strife. 4) A repudiation of international co-operation.**

_____ **2.** **The basic reason for labor strife in the postwar era was 1) the Communist influence in the ranks of organized labor 2) the attempt to organize the mass-production industries 3) the desire of labor to retain its wartime gains 4) the bitter rivalry between the A. F. of L. and the C.I.O.**

_____ **3.** **The Taft-Hartley Act 1) was neither as bad as its critics claimed nor as effective as its supporters contended 2) ruined the position of labor 3) earned Senator Taft labor's support 4) guaranteed the success of collective bargaining.**

_____ **4.** **One reason for the absence of disillusionment after World War II as compared to the disillusion after World War I was 1) that World War II was not as total a conflict 2) because the objectives of World War II were obtained 3) that World War II was fought in a more practical and realistic spirit 4) that there were fewer controls on the home front during World War II.**

_____ **5.** **Racial equality was NOT aided by 1) the passage of a national FEPC bill 2) the passage of many state FEPC bills 3) the decisions of the Supreme Court 4) the growth of a realization that second-class citizenship was incompatible with the principles of democracy.**

_____ **6.** **The immediate postwar years were marked by 1) chronic unemployment 2) greater stability of the American home 3) continued economic progress 4) extreme difficulties experienced by most veterans in adjusting to civilian life.**

_____ **7.** **The Republicans scored their greatest gains in the election of 1) 1944 2) 1946 3) 1948 4) 1950.**

_____ **8.** **The most unusual feature of the election of 1948 was that 1) the Republicans lost 2) there was a third party in the field 3) the Republican candidate had been previously defeated 4) pre-election forecasts proved wrong.**

_____ **9.** **NOT true of the 1948 election was that 1) Truman's folksy mannerisms had wide popular appeal 2) Dewey was cold and reserved 3) the nation was seeking conservative leadership 4) the margin of victory was small.**

_____ **10.** **Harry S. Truman was not distinguished by his 1) animosity toward the regular politicians of his party 2) successful work as an investigating senator 3) support of New Deal policies 4) sponsorship of reform measures.**

Essay Questions:

1. There has always been a difficult period of readjustment for the nation's economy after every war in American history. Why should the readjustment period after World War II have been so complex as compared with this period after other wars?

2. Why did organized labor provoke so much controversy after the war? What steps might have been taken to prevent this controversy?

3. What were the provisions of the Taft-Hartley Act? Was it just to describe it as a "slave labor bill"?

4. Describe the basic changes taking place in America in the immediate postwar period.

5. Why was Harry Truman's taking over the presidency especially difficult? What were the accomplishments of Truman in his first years in the White House?

6. Why was a Republican victory a seeming certainty in 1948? Account for Truman's surprising victory.

Terms, Events, and Personalities to Know:

Bill of Rights
Atomic Energy Commission
"G. I."
Thomas E. Dewey
Walter Reuther
Dixiecrats
General Motors strike
Progressive party
Korematsu **v** *United States*
FEPC

CHAPTER XXX

The Mirage of Peace

Summary:

Once the shooting was over, the American people anticipated a lasting peace. The ability of the Allies to co-operate during the war had built high hopes that such co-operation would continue into peacetime. However, the war was over but a short time before significant differences between the wartime allies appeared. A United Nations was created with more authority than the League of Nations had had, but this could not mask the basic power clash which emerged.

Peace was not realized in the postwar world principally because the Russians saw an opportunity to extend communism and to revive czarist imperialism as they sought to dominate eastern Europe. When President Truman realized that the Russians were intent upon extending their power he requested economic and military assistance for Turkey and Greece—the Truman Doctrine—thereby keeping those nations from falling behind the Iron Curtain. This was followed by the Marshall Plan, our effort to hold Berlin by means of the airlift in 1948, and the North Atlantic Treaty Organization, which securely committed America to the defense of Europe. In any event, there was no return to the isolationism that had followed World War I.

The situation in China was to provoke the greatest debate of the postwar period. Shortly after the war it was evident that Chiang Kai-shek's government did not have the support of the great majority of the Chinese people, and the communists quickly overran the country. Many Republicans attempted to blame the President for this disaster. In 1950 President Truman used American forces to aid the United Nations in an effort to stop the aggression in Korea.

Multiple Choice Questions:

_____ **1. Which of the following was NOT a cause of the postwar international conflict? 1) The revival of Russian imperialism. 2) The failure of American leaders to co-operate with the Russians. 3) The emergence of new revolutionary forces. 4) The power vacuum created by the fall of Germany and Japan.**

_____ **2. One significant difference between the United Nations and the League of Nations is that the UN 1) was divorced from the postwar treaties 2) was a grouping of sovereign states 3) was a product of compromise 4) had no affiliated court.**

_____ **3. The Yalta Conference was a failure because 1) Roosevelt surrendered to all of the Russian demands 2) Russian help was not needed against Japan 3) the veto power was granted to members of the Security Council 4) Russia failed to carry out her part of the commitments.**

_____ **4. Bernard Baruch made a significant contribution 1) as one of Truman's ambassadors to Russia 2) with his proposals to control atomic energy 3) in drafting the United Nations Charter 4) by drafting the Marshall Plan.**

_____ **5. The Truman Doctrine was intended to 1) aid in the holding of free elections in eastern Europe 2) keep China from going Communist 3) aid Greece and Turkey in their fight against Communism 4) assist Poland in her clash with Russia.**

______ **6.** **In his efforts to contain Communism, President Truman was least successful in 1) Japan 2) China 3) Berlin 4) Greece.**

______ **7.** **A vigorous critic of Truman's foreign policy was 1) George C. Marshall 2) Dean Acheson 3) Douglas MacArthur 4) Arthur Vandenberg.**

______ **8.** **President Roosevelt was NOT a member of the conference held at 1) Teheran 2) Potsdam 3) Yalta 4) Casablanca.**

______ **9.** **The basic objective of the Marshall Plan was to 1) provide military aid to nations fighting Communism 2) help Chiang Kai-shek fight Communism 3) help Europe revive economically 4) keep Berlin out of Russia's hands.**

______ **10.** **The long-range significance of Truman's intervention in Korea was that 1) Communism was dealt a severe defeat 2) American troops defeated the Chinese Communists 3) an effort had been made to halt overt aggression in the name of the UN 4) the Russians failed to veto the intervention.**

Essay Questions:

1. Why did the wartime alliance between Russia and the West disintegrate in the postwar period? What were the two distinct aspects of this conflict?

2. In setting up the United Nations, how did Roosevelt hope to avoid the mistakes of Wilson?

3. What were the primary decisions reached at Yalta? Upon what basis might these decisions be criticized? On what basis were these decisions justified?

4. Describe the main features of the United Nations. Why did it have difficulty at once? In what ways did the United Nations perform a real service immediately?

5. Discuss the steps taken by Russia after the war that increased the tension with the West.

6. What was the Truman Doctrine expected to accomplish? How effective did it prove in the long run?

7. Evaluate the success of the Marshall Plan as a means of checking the advance of Communism.

8. What caused the Berlin airlift? To what extent could it be said to have been a victory for the West?

9. Did the North Atlantic Treaty Organization hurt the strength of the United Nations? How was it a departure from typical American foreign policy?

10. What steps could have been taken to prevent the Communists from taking over China? Would the nation have supported President Truman in such a program?

11. Describe the background of the Korean War. Why was the intervention of the United Nations an historic step?

12. Present both sides of the argument in the Great Debate. Which side do you feel was right? Justify your answer.

Terms, Events, and Personalities to Know:

Bernard M. Baruch
Chiang Kai-shek
Potsdam Conference
"privileged sanctuary"
containment policy
Nuremburg Trials
ECA
thirty-eighth parallel
Secretariat
James F. Byrnes
UNRRA
People's Republic of China

CHAPTER XXXI

The Eisenhower Era

Summary:

In 1952 the Democrats could look back upon five straight triumphs in the election contests for President. After having been certain of victory in 1948 and then having lost, the Republicans wanted a sure winner in 1952. For this reason they passed over their leading candidate, Robert Taft of Ohio, and selected General Eisenhower. Eisenhower had a tremendous reputation as a military leader and diplomat and had not been associated with politics. His victory was assured, but the narrow majority by which the Republicans won control of Congress indicated that the people were voting for a person rather than for a party. The new administration represented a moderate shift toward conservatism and was prepared to accept a greater measure of influence from business than had the Democrats.

Eisenhower had to concern himself with the settlement of Korea, the problem of what to with Senator McCarthy, and the segregation issue. In 1956 Eisenhower was an easy victor again over Governor Stevenson of Illinois. However, only in 1952 were the Republicans able to control Congress. The people might vote for Eisenhower, but they still preferred Democrats in Congress.

In many respects the 1950's were similar to the 1920's. There was the same emphasis on materialism. Numerous new industries sparked the economy. Television performed a role comparable to that of radio in the earlier decade. The generation of the 1950's, however, was not revolting against anything. It was a generation that stressed uniformity and acceptance of the established order.

Multiple Choice Questions:

_____ 1. The best explanation of General Eisenhower's presidential victory in 1952 is 1) popular desire to repudiate twenty years of Democratic rule 2) the personal popularity of the Republican candidate 3) the inability of the Democratic candidate to campaign effectively 4) the extensive revelations of corruption in the national government.

_____ 2. Stevenson's running mate on the Democratic ticket in 1952 was 1) John Sparkman 2) Alben Barkley 3) Estes Kefauver 4) Sam Rayburn.

_____ 3. The basic reason why the GOP rejected Senator Taft as their nominee in 1952 was that 1) they feared Taft did not really represent the basic principles of the Republicans 2) his ill health made his election doubtful 3) he lacked support in the Midwest 4) they feared he could not be elected President.

_____ 4. In which of the following elections were the Republicans able to gain control of Congress? 1) 1952 2) 1954 3) 1956 4) 1958.

_____ 5. Which of the following cabinet members is not associated with his proper post? 1) Dulles—State 2) Wilson—Treasury 3) Durkin—Labor 4) Benson—Agriculture.

_____ 6. Senator McCarthy had his greatest appeal among 1) the nation's intellectuals 2) the pro-Communist element 3) those who really sought the truth 4) those who were seeking a scapegoat for the ills of the day.

_____ 7. Senator McCarthy's national prominence was terminated when 1) President Eisenhower repudiated his support 2) he claimed that the State Department harbored Communists 3) he attacked the integrity of former President Truman 4) he sought to discredit the United States Army.

_____ 8. When the Supreme Court decided that "separate but equal" educational facilities were unconstitutional they justified their action on the grounds that 1) the Fifth Amendment was being violated 2) the Fourteenth Amendment was being violated 3) there was a violation of the Bill of Rights 4) the federal government could establish state educational standards.

_____ 9. The first and most dramatic challenge to the Supreme Court desegregation decision came in 1) Louisville 2) Atlanta 3) New Orleans 4) Little Rock.

_____ 10. The first head of the A. F. of L.—C.I.O. was 1) Dave Beck 2) Jimmy Hoffa 3) George Meany 4) Walter Reuther.

_____ 11. A measure advocated for years and of far-reaching importance to the nation's economy and finally passed during the Eisenhower administration was 1) the offshore oil bill 2) a measure strengthening public power 3) a bill to unify the armed services 4) a bill to establish the St. Lawrence Seaway.

_____ 12. Which of the following was NOT caused by the rapid growth of the TV industry? 1) A far-reaching alteration in the production of movies. 2) A change in advertising techniques. 3) A change in political campaigning. 4) A decline in reading on the part of the general public.

_____ 13. Which of the following was NOT in the literary spotlight during the 1950's? 1) Leonard Bernstein 2) William Faulkner 3) John Steinbeck 4) Ernest Hemingway.

_____ 14. Which of the following was NOT an outstanding architect of the 1950's? 1) Eero Saarinen 2) Buckminster Fuller 3) Edward D. Stone 4) Louis Sullivan.

_____ 15. Congressional liberals differed with President Eisenhower especially over his stand on 1) raising the minimum wage 2) public electric power 3) integration 4) the broadening of Social Security coverage.

Essay Questions:

1. What qualities made General Eisenhower more desirable than Senator Taft as a Republican presidential candidate?

2. Why did Governor Stevenson have a wide following in 1952? To which group of voters did he have the strongest appeal?

3. How did the Eisenhower administration differ from the Roosevelt and Truman administrations? How was it similar?

4. To what extent may it be claimed that the Eisenhower administration scored a victory in the Korean peace settlement?

5. Can the South's resistance to the Supreme Court decision on integration be justified? In what ways can it not be justified?

6. What problems did organized labor face in the 1950's?

7. "A comparison between the 1920's and the 1950's is irrefutable proof that history does repeat itself." Discuss the accuracy of this quotation.

8. What were the basic characteristics of American cultural expression in the 1950's?

9. Compare and contrast Eisenhower and Truman as presidents. Why did Eisenhower's popularity continue after he was in office?

Terms, Events, and Personalities to Know:

"Mr. Republican"
Adlai E. Stevenson
Charles E. Wilson
George M. Humphrey
Martin P. Durkin
John Foster Dulles
"agonizing reappraisal"
"brink of war"
38th parallel
Joseph R. McCarthy
Alger Hiss
Whittaker Chambers
McCarran Act
"separate but equal"
Brown v *Board of Education of Topeka*
NAACP
George Meany
Walter Reuther
offshore oil rights
St. Lawrence Seaway
Leonard Bernstein

CHAPTER XXXII

America and the World

Summary:

The difficult international situation the Eisenhower administration inherited continued unchanged through the period from 1953 to 1958. The first challenge occurred in Indochina, where France found itself unable to continue a costly war. The United States was asked for assistance, and when it was not forthcoming the French made a compromise with the communists which turned over northern Vietnam to them. An attempt to settle many of the outstanding differences between Russia and the United States was made at Geneva, where President Eisenhower met the Russian leaders. Unfortunately, the "spirit of Geneva" proved to be of short duration and of no significance. The possibility of a conflict with communist China remained largely because of the American defense of the Chiang Kai-shek regime on Formosa. In the fall of 1956 the United States faced a major crisis when Great Britain and France joined Israel in an attack on Egypt in an effort to regain the Suez Canal. At approximately the same time Hungary revolted against Russian tyranny, but the United States took no action. American prestige was dealt a serious blow in the fall of 1957 when Sputnik was launched. This triumph stressed the fact that Russian scientific attainments were far more important than had previously been believed. In 1958 the threat of world communism was as strong as at any time in the postwar era.

Multiple Choice Questions:

______ **1. SEATO was 1) supported by India 2) more effective than NATO 3) a formal military alliance created to protect Asia from Communism 4) a graphic illustration of American commitments in the Orient.**

______ **2. The European Defense Community 1) was able to create an international army for the defense of NATO 2) virtually collapsed when France failed to support it 3) was supported by Russia 4) represented a triumph for American policy.**

_____ 3. The "Spirit of Geneva" 1) was a major triumph for Eisenhower's foreign policy 2) ended the cold war 3) was of short duration 4) grew out of events immediately after Stalin's death.

_____ 4. The basic issue between the United States and Communist China grew out of 1) American assistance to Nationalist China 2) Communist atrocities in Tibet 3) the blockade activity of the American Seventh Fleet 4) the status of Formosa.

_____ 5. The United States and Russia collaborated in 1) suppressing the revolt in Hungary 2) backing Israel's invasion of Egypt 3) opposing English-French seizure of Suez 4) the invasion of Lebanon.

_____ 6. The Eisenhower Doctrine 1) was a pledge of aid to the Middle East to check Communist penetration 2) led to the unleashing of Chiang Kai-shek 3) committed the United States to the defense of Quemoy and Matsu 4) bolstered NATO.

_____ 7. Nasser was the militant nationalist leader of 1) Iran 2) Turkey 3) Jordan 4) Egypt.

_____ 8. Russia's domination of eastern Europe was challenged in 1956 when 1) Tito revolted 2) Hungary arose in revolt 3) riots swept East Berlin 4) the Poles engaged in a bloody uprising.

_____ 9. To most Americans Sputnik was important because it 1) proved Russia to be far ahead in the arms race 2) represented a triumph for the Eisenhower administration 3) showed that the Soviet Union had more scientific and technical ability than had been realized 4) proved that Soviet technical education was superior to that in America.

_____ 10. The election results in 1958 1) were a personal triumph for President Eisenhower 2) reflected a growing surge of Republican strength 3) enabled the Republicans to recapture the House but not the Senate 4) indicated much dissatisfaction with the leadership qualities of the Eisenhower administration.

Essay Questions:

1. What lessons were learned by the West at the Geneva Conference?

2. Why was there a controversy between the United States and Communist China in the 1950's? What are the arguments in favor of recognition of the Communist regime in China? What are the arguments against such recognition?

3. Why did the Hungarian uprising in 1956 create so much interest in the Western world?

4. What caused the English-French intervention in Suez in 1956? Was the co-operation of the United States with Russia in this instance the proper course of action?

5. What were the implications of Sputnik?

6. Why was the decade of the 1950's a difficult one for the American people in terms of foreign affairs?

Terms, Events, and Personalities to Know:

Christian Herter
Warsaw Pact
SEATO
Seventh Fleet
Point Four
Quemoy
Gamal Abdul Nasser
Matsu
"Spirit of Geneva"
Imre Nagy
Wladyslaw Gomulka
Aswan Dam
Eisenhower Doctrine

Answers to Multiple Choice Questions

Chapter I
1 — **3**
2 — **4**
3 — **3**
4 — **4**
5 — **1**
6 — **4**
7 — **1**
8 — **3**
9 — **3**

Chapter II
1 — **4**
2 — **2**
3 — **3**
4 — **1**
5 — **3**
6 — **2**
7 — **4**
8 — **3**
9 — **1**
10 — **3**

Chapter III
1 — **4**
2 — **1**
3 — **3**
4 — **3**
5 — **4**
6 — **3**
7 — **2**
8 — **4**
9 — **2**

Chapter IV
1 — **3**
2 — **4**
3 — **4**
4 — **3**
5 — **1**
6 — **4**
7 — **1**
8 — **3**
9 — **2**
10 — **4**

Chapter V
1 — **1**
2 — **3**
3 — **3**
4 — **2**
5 — **4**
6 — **4**
7 — **3**
8 — **2**
9 — **4**
10 — **4**

Chapter VI
1 — **2**
2 — **2**
3 — **4**
4 — **3**
5 — **4**
6 — **4**
7 — **2**
8 — **4**

Chapter VII
1 — **4**
2 — **2**
3 — **3**
4 — **3**
5 — **1**
6 — **3**
7 — **2**
8 — **3**
9 — **4**
10 — **2**

Chapter VIII
1 — **3**
2 — **1**
3 — **3**
4 — **4**
5 — **3**
6 — **2**
7 — **1**
8 — **3**
9 — **2**
10 — **4**

Chapter IX
1 — **1**
2 — **3**
3 — **4**
4 — **1**
5 — **3**
6 — **4**
7 — **3**
8 — **2**
9 — **3**
10 — **4**

Chapter X
1 — **3**
2 — **4**
3 — **2**
4 — **3**
5 — **3**
6 — **2**
7 — **4**
8 — **3**
9 — **3**
10 — **4**

Chapter XI
1 — **3**
2 — **4**
3 — **2**
4 — **1**
5 — **2**
6 — **4**
7 — **2**
8 — **1**
9 — **2**
10 — **3**

Chapter XII
1 — **2**
2 — **3**
3 — **1**
4 — **3**
5 — **4**
6 — **2**
7 — **2**
8 — **4**
9 — **4**
10 — **3**

Chapter XIII
1 — **2**
2 — **3**
3 — **4**
4 — **2**
5 — **4**
6 — **2**
7 — **3**
8 — **4**

Chapter XIV
1 — **2**
2 — **4**
3 — **1**
4 — **4**
5 — **3**
6 — **4**
7 — **3**
8 — **2**
9 — **3**
10 — **3**

Chapter XV
1 — **2**
2 — **2**
3 — **3**
4 — **3**
5 — **2**
6 — **1**
7 — **4**
8 — **2**
9 — **4**
10 — **3**

Chapter XVI
1 — **4**
2 — **2**
3 — **4**
4 — **2**
5 — **3**
6 — **4**
7 — **3**
8 — **2**
9 — **1**
10 — **1**

Chapter XVII
1 — **4**
2 — **2**
3 — **4**
4 — **2**
5 — **4**
6 — **1**
7 — **3**
8 — **4**
9 — **3**
10 — **4**

Chapter XVIII
1 — **4**
2 — **3**
3 — **1**
4 — **1**
5 — **2**
6 — **2**
7 — **1**
8 — **2**
9 — **3**
10 — **4**

Chapter XIX
1 — **4**
2 — **2**
3 — **3**
4 — **2**
5 — **3**
6 — **2**
7 — **1**
8 — **3**
9 — **3**
10 — **3**

Chapter XX
1 — **3**
2 — **2**
3 — **1**
4 — **4**
5 — **3**
6 — **4**
7 — **2**
8 — **3**
9 — **2**
10 — **4**

Chapter XXI
1 — **3**
2 — **2**
3 — **4**
4 — **4**
5 — **3**
6 — **3**
7 — **1**
8 — **4**
9 — **4**
10 — **4**

Chapter XXII
1 — **1**
2 — **4**
3 — **2**
4 — **3**
5 — **2**
6 — **2**
7 — **3**
8 — **2**
9 — **1**
10 — **3**

Chapter XXIII
1 — **2**
2 — **3**
3 — **3**
4 — **4**
5 — **2**
6 — **4**
7 — **1**

Chapter XXIV
1 — **3**
2 — **2**
3 — **4**
4 — **3**
5 — **4**
6 — **2**
7 — **2**
8 — **3**
9 — **1**
10 — **4**

Chapter XXV
1 — **2**
2 — **4**
3 — **3**
4 — **2**
5 — **4**
6 — **2**
7 — **4**
8 — **3**
9 — **2**
10 — **3**

Chapter XXVI
1 — **4**
2 — **2**
3 — **3**
4 — **4**
5 — **1**
6 — **1**
7 — **3**
8 — **2**
9 — **4**
10 — **4**

Chapter XXVII
1 — **2**
2 — **3**
3 — **4**
4 — **1**
5 — **4**
6 — **2**
7 — **3**
8 — **3**
9 — **1**
10 — **2**

Chapter XXVIII
1 — **3**
2 — **3**
3 — **2**
4 — **1**
5 — **4**
6 — **3**
7 — **4**
8 — **3**
9 — **2**
10 — **2**

Chapter XXIX
1 — **4**
2 — **3**
3 — **1**
4 — **3**
5 — **1**
6 — **3**
7 — **2**
8 — **4**
9 — **3**
10 — **1**

Chapter XXX
1 — **2**
2 — **1**
3 — **4**
4 — **2**
5 — **3**
6 — **2**
7 — **3**
8 — **2**
9 — **3**
10 — **3**

Chapter XXXI
1 — **2**
2 — **1**
3 — **4**
4 — **1**
5 — **2**
6 — **4**
7 — **4**
8 — **2**
9 — **4**
10 — **3**
11 — **4**
12 — **4**
13 — **1**
14 — **4**
15 — **2**

Chapter XXXII
1 — **4**
2 — **2**
3 — **3**
4 — **4**
5 — **3**
6 — **1**
7 — **4**
8 — **2**
9 — **3**
10 — **4**

Appendices

APPENDIX A

The Declaration of Independence

In Congress, July 4, 1776
The Unanimous Declaration of the Thirteen United States of America

When, in the Course of human events, it becomes necessary for one people to dissolve the political bands which have connected them with another, and to assume among the powers of the earth, the separate and equal station to which the Laws of Nature and of Nature's God entitle them, a decent respect to the opinions of mankind requires that they should declare the causes which impel them to the separation.

We hold these truths to be self-evident, that all men are created equal, that they are endowed by their Creator with certain unalienable Rights, that among these, are Life, Liberty, and the pursuit of Happiness. That, to secure these rights, Governments are instituted among Men, deriving their just powers from the consent of the governed, that, whenever any Form of Government becomes destructive of these ends, it is the Right of the People to alter or to abolish it, and to institute new Government, laying its foundation on such principles, and organizing its powers in such form, as to them shall seem most likely to effect their Safety and Happiness. Prudence, indeed, will dictate that Governments long established, should not be changed for light and transient causes; and, accordingly, all experience hath shewn, that mankind are more disposed to suffer, while evils are sufferable, than to right themselves by abolishing the forms to which they are accustomed. But, when a long train of abuses and usurpations, pursuing invariably the same Object, evinces a design to reduce them under absolute Despotism, it is their right, it is their duty, to throw off such Government and to provide new Guards for their future security.—Such has been the patient sufferance of these Colonies; and such is now the necessity which constrains them to alter their former Systems of Government. The history of the present King of Great Britain is a history of repeated injuries and usurpations, all having in direct object the establishment of an absolute Tyranny over these States. To prove this, let Facts be submitted to a candid world.—

He has refused his Assent to Laws the most wholesome and necessary for the public good.

He has forbidden his Governors to pass Laws of immediate and pressing importance, unless suspended in their operation till his Assent should be obtained; and when so suspended, he has utterly neglected to attend to them.

He has refused to pass other laws for the accommodation of large districts of people, unless those people would relinquish the right of Representation in the Legislature; a right inestimable to them and formidable to tyrants only.

He has called together legislative bodies at places unusual, uncomfortable, and distant from the depository of their public Records, for the sole purpose of fatiguing them into compliance with his measures.

He has dissolved Representative Houses repeatedly, for opposing with manly firmness his invasions on the rights of the people.

He has refused for a long time, after such dissolutions, to cause others to be elected; whereby the Legislative powers, incapable of Annihilation, have returned to the People at large for their exercise; the State remaining, in the meantime, exposed to all the dangers of invasion from without, and convulsions within.

He has endeavored to prevent the population of these States; for that purpose, obstructing the Laws for Naturalization of Foreigners; refusing to pass others to encourage their migrations hither, and raising the conditions of new Appropriations of Lands.

He has obstructed the Administration of Justice, by refusing his Assent to Laws for establishing Judiciary powers.

He has made Judges dependent on his Will alone, for the tenure of their offices, and the amount and payment of their salaries.

He has erected a multitude of New Offices, and sent hither swarms of Officers to harass our people, and eat out their substance.

He has kept among us, in times of peace, Standing Armies, without the Consent of our legislatures.

He has affected to render the Military independent of, and superior to, the Civil power.

He has combined, with others, to subject us to a jurisdiction foreign to our constitution, and unacknowledged by our laws; giving his Assent to their Acts of pretended Legislation:

For quartering large bodies of armed troops among us:

For protecting them by a mock Trial, from punishment, for any Murders which they should commit on the Inhabitants of these States:

For cutting off our Trade with all parts of the world:

For imposing Taxes on us without our Consent:

For depriving us, in many cases, of the benefits of Trial by Jury:

For transporting us beyond Seas to be tried for pretended offenses:

For abolishing the free System of English Laws in a neighboring Province, establishing therein an Arbitrary government, and enlarging its Boundaries, so as to render it at once an example and fit instrument for introducing the same absolute rule into these Colonies:

For taking away our Charters, abolishing our most valuable Laws, and altering, fundamentally, the Forms of our Governments:

For suspending our own Legislatures, and declaring themselves invested with power to legislate for us in all cases whatsoever.

He has abdicated Government here, by declaring us out of his Protection, and waging War against us.

He has plundered our seas, ravaged our Coasts, burnt our towns, and destroyed the lives of our people.

He is, at this time, transporting large Armies of foreign Mercenaries to compleat the works of death, desolation, and tyranny, already begun with circumstances of Cruelty & perfidy scarcely paralleled in the most barbarous ages, and totally unworthy the Head of a civilized nation.

He has constrained our fellow Citizens, taken Captive on the high Seas, to bear Arms against their Country, to become the executioners of their friends and Brethren, or to fall themselves by their Hands.

He has excited domestic insurrections amongst us, and has endeavored to bring on the inhabitants of our frontiers, the merciless Indian Savages, whose known rule of warfare, is an undistinguished destruction of all ages, sexes and conditions.

In every stage of these Oppressions, We have Petitioned for Redress, in the most humble terms; our repeated Petitions have been answered only by repeated injury. A Prince, whose character is thus marked by every act which may define a Tyrant, is unfit to be the ruler of a free people.

Nor have we been wanting in attentions to our British brethren. We have warned them, from time to time, of attempts made by their legislature to extend an unwarrantable jurisdiction over us. We have reminded them of the circumstances of our emigration and settlement here. We have appealed to their native justice and magnanimity, and we have conjured them by the ties of our common kindred to disavow these usurpations, which would inevitably interrupt our connections and correspondence. They too have been deaf to the voice of justice and of consanguinity. We must, therefore, acquiesce in the necessity, which denounces our Separation, and hold them, as we hold the rest of mankind, Enemies in War, in Peace Friends.

We, therefore, the Representatives of the united States of America, in General Congress, Assembled, appealing to the Supreme Judge of the world for the rectitude of our intentions, do. in the Name, and by Authority of the good People of these Colonies, solemnly publish and declare, That these United Colonies are, and of Right ought to be, Free and Independent States; that they are Absolved from all Allegiance to the British Crown, and that all political connection between them and the State of Great Britain is, and ought to be, totally dissolved: and that, as Free and Independent States, they have full Power to levy War, conclude Peace, contract Alliances, establish Commerce, and to do all other Acts and Things which Independent States may of right do. And, for the support of this Declaration, with a firm reliance on the protection of divine Providence, we mutually pledge to each other our Lives, our Fortunes, and our sacred Honor.

The foregoing Declaration was, by order of Congress, engrossed, and signed by the following members:

John Hancock

NEW HAMPSHIRE

Josiah Bartlett
William Whipple
Matthew Thornton

MASSACHUSETTS BAY

Samuel Adams
John Adams
Robert Treat Paine
Elbridge Gerry

RHODE ISLAND

Stephen Hopkins
William Ellery

CONNECTICUT

Roger Sherman
Samuel Huntington
William Williams
Oliver Wolcott

NEW YORK

William Floyd
Philip Livingston
Francis Lewis
Lewis Morris

NEW JERSEY

Richard Stockton
John Witherspoon
Francis Hopkinson
John Hart
Abraham Clark

PENNSYLVANIA

Robert Morris
Benjamin Rush
Benjamin Franklin
John Morton
George Clymer
James Smith
George Taylor
James Wilson
George Ross

DELAWARE

Caesar Rodney
George Read
Thomas M'Kean

MARYLAND

Samuel Chase
William Paca
Thomas Stone
Charles Carroll, of Carrollton

VIRGINIA

George Wythe
Richard Henry Lee
Thomas Jefferson
Benjamin Harrison
Thomas Nelson, Jr.
Francis Lightfoot Lee
Carter Braxton

NORTH CAROLINA

William Hooper
Joseph Hewes
John Penn

SOUTH CAROLINA

Edward Rutledge
Thomas Heyward, Jr.
Thomas Lynch, Jr.
Arthur Middleton

GEORGIA

Button Gwinnett
Lyman Hall
George Walton

RESOLVED, That copies of the Declaration be sent to the several assemblies, conventions, and committees, or councils of safety, and to the several commanding officers of the continental troops; that it be proclaimed in each of the united States, at the head of the army.

APPENDIX B

The Constitution of the United States

WE THE PEOPLE of the United States, in Order to form a more perfect Union, establish Justice, insure domestic Tranquility, provide for the common defence, promote the general Welfare, and secure the Blessings of Liberty to ourselves and our Posterity, do ordain and establish this CONSTITUTION for the United States of America.

ARTICLE I.

Section 1. All legislative Powers herein granted shall be vested in a Congress of the United States, which shall consist of a Senate and House of Representatives.

Section 2. The House of Representatives shall be composed of Members chosen every second Year by the People of the several States, and the Electors in each State shall have the Qualifications requisite for Electors of the most numerous Branch of the State Legislature.

No Person shall be a Representative who shall not have attained to the Age of twenty-five Years, and been seven Years a Citizen of the United States, and who shall not, when elected, be an Inhabitant of that State in which he shall be chosen.

(Representatives and direct Taxes shall be apportioned among the several States which may be included within this Union, according to their respective Numbers, which shall be determined by adding to the whole Number of free Persons, including those bound to Service for a Term of Years, and excluding Indians not taxed, three fifths of all other Persons.) The actual Enumeration shall be made within three Years after the first Meeting of the Congress of the United States, and within every subsequent Term of ten Years, in such Manner as they shall by Law direct. The Number of Representatives shall not exceed one for every thirty Thousand, but each State shall have at Least one Representative; and until such enumeration shall be made, the State of New Hampshire shall be entitled to chuse three, Massachusetts eight, Rhode-Island and Providence Plantations one, Connecticut five, New-York six, New Jersey four, Pennsylvania eight, Delaware one, Maryland six, Virginia ten, North Carolina five, South Carolina five, and Georgia three.

When vacancies happen in the Representation from any State, the Executive Authority thereof shall issue Writs of Election to fill such Vacancies.

The House of Representatives shall chuse their Speaker and other Officers; and shall have the sole Power of Impeachment.

Section 3. The Senate of the United States shall be composed of two Senators from each State, chosen by the Legislature thereof, for six Years; and each Senator shall have one Vote.

Immediately after they shall be assembled in Consequence of the first Election, they shall be divided as equally as may be into three Classes. The Seats of the Senators of the first Class shall be vacated at the Expiration of the Second Year, of the second Class at the Expiration of the fourth Year, and of the third Class at the Expiration of the sixth Year, so that one-third may be chosen every second Year; and if Vacancies happen by Resignation, or otherwise, during the Recess of the Legislature of any State, the Executive thereof may make temporary Appointments until the next Meeting of the Legislature, which shall then fill such Vacancies.

No Person shall be a Senator who shall not have attained to the Age of thirty Years, and been nine Years a Citizen of the United States, and who shall not, when elected, be an Inhabitant of that State for which he shall be chosen.

The Vice President of the United States shall be President of the Senate, but shall have no vote, unless they be equally divided.

The Senate shall chuse their other Officers, and also a President pro tempore, in the absence of the Vice President, or when he shall exercise the Office of President of the United States.

The Senate shall have the sole Power to try all Impeachments. When sitting for that purpose, they shall be on Oath or Affirmation. When the President of the United States is tried, the Chief Justice shall preside: And no person shall be convicted without the Concurrence of two thirds of the Members present.

Judgment in Cases of Impeachment shall not extend further than to removal from Office, and disqualification to hold and enjoy any Office of honor, Trust, or Profit under the United States: but the Party convicted shall nevertheless be liable and subject to Indictment, Trial, Judgment, and Punishment, according to Law.

Section 4. The Times, Places and Manner of holding Elections for Senators and Representatives, shall be prescribed in each State by the Legislature thereof; but the Congress may at any time by Law make or alter such Regulations, except as to the Places of Chusing Senators.

The Congress shall assemble at least once in every Year, and such Meeting shall be on the first Monday in December, unless they shall by Law appoint a different Day.

Section 5. Each House shall be the Judge of the Elections, Returns and Qualifications of its own Members, and a Majority of each shall constitute a Quorum to do Business; but a smaller number may adjourn from day to day, and may be authorized to compel the Attendance of absent Members, in such Manner, and under such Penalties, as each House may provide.

Each House may determine the Rules of its Proceedings, punish its Members for disorderly Behavior, and, with the Concurrence of two thirds, expel a Member.

Each House shall keep a Journal of its Proceedings, and from time to time publish the same, excepting such Parts as may in their Judgment require Secrecy; and the Yeas and Nays of the Members of either House on any question shall, at the Desire of one fifth of those Present, be entered on the Journal.

Neither House, during the Session of Congress, shall, without the Consent of the other, adjourn for more than three days, nor to any other Place than that in which the two Houses shall be sitting.

Section 6. The Senators and Representatives shall receive a Compensation for their Services, to be ascertained by Law, and paid out of the Treasury of the United States. They shall in all Cases, except Treason, Felony, and Breach of the Peace, be privileged from Arrest during their Attendance at the Session of their respective Houses, and in going to and returning from the same; and for any Speech or Debate in either House, they shall not be questioned in any other Place.

No Senator or Representative shall, during the Time for which he was elected, be appointed to any civil Office under the Authority of the United States, which shall have been created, or the Emoluments whereof shall have been increased, during such time; and no Person holding any Office under the United States shall be a Member of either House during his continuance in Office.

Section 7. All Bills for raising Revenue shall originate in the House of Representatives; but the Senate may propose or concur with Amendments as on other bills.

Every Bill which shall have passed the House of Representatives and the Senate, shall, before it become a law, be presented to the President of the United States; If he approve he shall sign it, but if not he shall return it, with his Objections, to that House in which it shall have originated, who shall enter the Objections at large on their Journal, and proceed to reconsider it. If after such Reconsideration two thirds of that House shall agree to pass the bill, it shall be sent, together with the objections, to the other House, by which it shall likewise be reconsidered, and if approved by two thirds of that House, it shall become a Law. But in all such Cases the Votes of both Houses shall be determined by Yeas and Nays, and the Names of the Persons voting for and against the Bill shall be entered on the Journal of each House respectively. If any Bill shall not be returned by the President within ten Days (Sundays excepted) after it shall have been presented to him, the Same shall be a

Law, in like Manner as if he had signed it, unless the Congress by their Adjournment prevent its Return, in which Case it shall not be a Law.

Every Order, Resolution, or Vote to which the Concurrence of the Senate and House of Representatives may be necessary (except on a question of Adjournment) shall be presented to the President of the United States; and before the Same shall take Effect, shall be approved by him, or being disapproved by him, shall be repassed by two thirds of the Senate and House of Representatives, according to the Rules and Limitations prescribed in the Case of a Bill.

Section 8. The Congress shall have Power To lay and collect Taxes, Duties, Imposts and Excises, to pay the Debts and provide for the common Defence and general Welfare of the United States; but all Duties, Imposts and Excises shall be uniform throughout the United States;

To borrow money on the credit of the United States;

To regulate Commerce with foreign Nations, and among the several States, and with the Indian Tribes;

To establish an uniform Rule of Naturalization, and uniform Laws on the subject of Bankruptcies throughout the United States;

To coin Money, regulate the Value thereof, and of foreign Coin, and fix the Standard of Weights and Measures;

To provide for the Punishment of counterfeiting the Securities and current Coin of the United States;

To establish Post Offices and post Roads;

To promote the Progress of Science and useful Arts, by securing for limited Times to Authors and Inventors the exclusive Right to their respective Writings and Discoveries;

To constitute Tribunals inferior to the Supreme Court;

To define and punish Piracies and Felonies committed on the high Seas, and Offenses against the Law of Nations;

To declare War, grant Letters of Marque and Reprisal, and make Rules concerning Captures on Land and Water;

To raise and support Armies, but no Appropriation of Money to that Use shall be for a longer Term than two Years;

To provide and maintain a Navy;

To make Rules for the Government and Regulation of the land and naval forces;

To provide for calling forth the Militia to execute the Laws of the Union, suppress Insurrections and repel Invasions;

To provide for organizing, arming, and disciplining the Militia, and for governing such Part of them as may be employed in the Service of the United States, reserving to the States respectively, the Appointment of the Officers, and the Authority of training the Militia according to the discipline prescribed by Congress;

To exercise exclusive Legislation in all Cases whatsoever, over such District (not exceeding ten Miles square) as may, by Cession of particular States, and the acceptance of Congress, become the Seat of the Government of the United States, and to exercise like Authority over all Places purchased by the Consent of the Legislature of the State in which the Same shall be, for the Erection of Forts, Magazines, Arsenals, dock-Yards, and other needful Buildings;—And

To make all Laws which shall be necessary and proper for carrying into Execution the foregoing Powers, and all other Powers vested by this Constitution in the Government of the United States, or in any Department or Officer thereof.

Section 9. The Migration or Importation of such Persons as any of the States now existing shall think proper to admit, shall not be prohibited by the Congress prior to the Year one thousand eight hundred and eight, but a tax or duty may be imposed on such Importation, not exceeding ten dollars for each Person.

The privilege of the Writ of Habeas Corpus shall not be suspended, unless when in Cases of Rebellion or Invasion the public Safety may require it.

No Bill of Attainder or ex post facto Law shall be passed.

No capitation, or other direct, Tax shall be laid unless in Proportion to the Census or Enumeration herein before directed to be taken.

No Tax or Duty shall be laid on Articles exported from any State.

No Preference shall be given by any Regulation of Commerce or Revenue to the Ports of one State over those of another; nor shall Vessels bound to, or from, one State, be obliged to enter, clear, or pay Duties in another.

No Money shall be drawn from the Treasury, but in Consequence of Appropriations made by Law; and a regular Statement and Account of the Receipts and Expenditures of all public Money shall be published from time to time.

No Title of Nobility shall be granted by the United States: And no Person holding any Office of Profit or Trust under them, shall, without the Consent of the Congress, accept of any present, Emolument, Office, or Title, of any kind whatever, from any King, Prince, or foreign State.

Section. 10. No State shall enter into any Treaty, Alliance, or Confederation; grant Letters of Marque and Reprisal; coin Money; emit Bills of Credit; make any Thing but gold and silver Coin or Tender in Payment of Debts; pass any Bill of Attainder, ex post facto Law, or Law impairing the Obligation of Contracts, or grant any Title of Nobility.

No State shall, without the Consent of the Congress, lay any Imposts or Duties on Imports or Exports, except what may be absolutely necessary for executing its inspection Laws: and the net Produce of all Duties and Imposts, laid by any State on Imports or Exports, shall be for the Use of the Treasury of the United States; and all such Laws shall be subject to the Revision and Controul of the Congress.

No State shall, without the Consent of Congress, lay any duty of Tonnage, keep Troops, or Ships of War in time of Peace, enter into any Agreement or Compact with another State, or with a foreign Power, or engage in War, unless actually invaded, or in such imminent Danger as will not admit of delay.

ARTICLE II.

Section 1. The executive power shall be vested in a President of the United States of America. He shall hold his Office during the Term of four years, and, together with the Vice-President, chosen for the same Term, be elected, as follows:

Each State shall appoint, in such Manner as the Legislature thereof may direct, a Number of Electors, equal to the whole Number of Senators and Representatives to which the State may be entitled in the Congress: but no Senator or Representative, or Person holding an Office of Trust or Profit under the United States, shall be appointed an Elector.

(The Electors shall meet in their respective States, and vote by Ballot for two persons, of whom one at least shall not be an Inhabitant of the same State with themselves. And they shall make a List of all the Persons voted for, and of the Number of Votes for each; which List they shall sign and certify, and transmit sealed to the Seat of the Government of the United States, directed to the President of the Senate. The President of the Senate shall, in the Presence of the Senate and House of Representatives, open all the Certificates, and the Votes shall then be counted. The Person having the greatest Number of Votes shall be the President, if such Number be a Majority of the whole Number of Electors appointed; and if there be more than one who have such Majority, and have an equal Number of Votes, then the House of Representatives shall immediately chuse by Ballot one of them for President; and if no Person have a Majority, then from the five highest on the List the said House shall in like Manner chuse the President. But in chusing the President, the Votes shall be taken by States, the Representation from each State having one Vote; a quorum for this Purpose shall consist of a Member or Members from two-thirds of the States, and a Majority of all the States shall be necessary to a Choice. In every Case, after the Choice of the President, the Person having the greatest Number of Votes of the Electors shall be the Vice President. But if there should remain two or more who have equal votes, the Senate shall chuse from them by Ballot the Vice-President.)

The Congress may determine the Time of chusing the Electors, and the Day on which they shall give their Votes; which Day shall be the same throughout the United States.

No person except a natural-born Citizen, or a Citizen of the United States, at the time of the Adoption of this Constitution, shall be eligible to the Office of President; neither shall any Person be eligible to that Office who shall not have attained to the Age of thirty-five years, and been fourteen Years a Resident within the United States.

In Case of the Removal of the President from Office, or of his Death, Resignation, or Inability to discharge the Powers and Duties of the said

Office, the same shall devolve on the Vice President, and the Congress may by Law provide for the Case of Removal, Death, Resignation, or Inability, both of the President and Vice President, declaring what Officer shall then act as President, and such Officer shall act accordingly, until the disability be removed, or a President shall be elected.

The President shall, at stated Times, receive for his Services a Compensation, which shall neither be increased nor diminished during the Period for which he shall have been elected, and he shall not receive within that Period any other Emolument from the United States, or any of them.

Before he enter on the execution of his Office, he shall take the following Oath or Affirmation:—"I do solemnly swear (or affirm) that I will faithfully execute the Office of President of the United States, and will, to the best of my Ability, preserve, protect, and defend the Constitution of the United States."

Section 2. The President shall be Commander in Chief of the Army and Navy of the United States, and of the Militia of the several States, when called into the actual Service of the United States; he may require the Opinion, in writing, of the principal Officer in each of the executive Departments, upon any subject relating to the Duties of their respective Offices, and he shall have Power to Grant Reprieves and Pardons for Offenses against the United States, except in Cases of Impeachment.

He shall have Power, by and with the Advice and Consent of the Senate, to make Treaties, provided two thirds of the Senators present concur; and he shall nominate, and by and with the Advice and Consent of the Senate, shall appoint Ambassadors, other public Ministers and Consuls, Judges of the supreme Court, and all other Officers of the United States, whose Appointments are not herein otherwise provided for, and which shall be established by Law: but the Congress may by Law vest the Appointment of such inferior Officers, as they think proper, in the President alone, in the Courts of Law, or in the Heads of Departments.

The President shall have Power to fill up all Vacancies that may happen during the Recess of the Senate, by granting Commissions which shall expire at the End of their next Session.

Section 3. He shall from time to time give to the Congress Information of the State of the Union, and recommend to their Consideration such Measures as he shall judge necessary and expedient; he may, on extraordinary occasions, convene both Houses, or either of them, and in Case of Disagreement between them, with respect to the Time of Adjournment, he may adjourn them to such Time as he shall think proper; he shall receive Ambassadors and other public Ministers; he shall take Care that the Laws be faithfully executed, and shall Commission all the Officers of the United States.

Section 4. The President, Vice President and all civil Officers of the United States, shall be removed from Office on Impeachment for, and Conviction of, Treason, Bribery, or other high Crimes and Misdemeanors.

ARTICLE III.

Section 1. The judicial Power of the United States, shall be vested in one supreme Court, and in such inferior Courts as the Congress may from time to time ordain and establish. The Judges, both of the supreme and inferior Courts, shall hold their Offices during good Behaviour, and shall, at stated Times, receive for their Services, a Compensation, which shall not be diminished during their Continuance in Office.

Section 2. The judicial Power shall extend to all Cases, in Law and Equity, arising under this Constitution, the Laws of the United States, and Treaties made or which shall be made, under their Authority;—to all Cases affecting ambassadors, other public ministers and consuls;—to all cases of admiralty and maritime Jurisdiction;—to Controversies to which the United States shall be a Party;—to Controversies between two or more States; between a State and Citizens of another State;—between Citizens of different States,—between Citizens of the same State claiming Lands under Grants of different States, and between a State, or the Citizens thereof, and foreign States, Citizens or Subjects.

In all Cases affecting Ambassadors, other public Ministers and Consuls, and those in which a State shall be Party, the supreme Court shall have original Jurisdiction. In all the other Cases before mentioned, the supreme Court shall have appellate Jurisdiction, both as to Law and Fact, with such Exceptions, and under such Regulations as the Congress shall make.

The trial of all Crimes, except in Cases of Impeachment, shall be by Jury; and such Trial shall be held in the State where the said Crimes shall have been committed; but when not committed within any State, the Trial shall be at such Place or Places as the Congress may by Law have directed.

Section 3. Treason against the United States, shall consist only in levying War against them, or in adhering to their Enemies, giving them Aid and Comfort. No Person shall be convicted of Treason unless on the Testimony of two Witnesses to the same overt Act, or on Confession in open Court.

The Congress shall have power to declare the Punishment of Treason, but no Attainder of Treason shall work Corruption of Blood, or Forfeiture except during the Life of the Person attainted.

ARTICLE IV.

Section 1. Full Faith and Credit shall be given in each State to the public Acts, Records, and judicial Proceedings of every other State. And the Congress may by general Laws prescribe the Manner in which such Acts, Records and Proceedings shall be proved, and the Effect thereof.

Section 2. The Citizens of each State shall be entitled to all Privileges and Immunities of Citizens in the several States.

A Person charged in any State with Treason, Felony, or other Crime, who shall flee from Justice, and be found in another State, shall on demand of the executive Authority of the State from which he fled, be delivered up, to be removed to the State having Jurisdiction of the crime.

No Person held to Service or Labour in one State, under the Laws thereof, escaping into another, shall, in Consequence of any Law or Regulation therein, be discharged from such Service or Labour, but shall be delivered up on Claim of the Party to whom such Service or Labour may be due.

Section 3. New States may be admitted by the Congress into this Union; but no new State shall be formed or erected within the Jurisdiction of any other State; nor any State be Formed by the Junction of two or more States, or parts of States, without the Consent of the Legislatures of the States concerned as well as of the Congress.

The Congress shall have Power to dispose of and make all needful Rules and Regulations respecting the Territory or other Property belonging to the United States; and nothing in this Constitution shall be so construed as to Prejudice any Claims of the United States, or of any particular State.

Section 4. The United States shall guarantee to every State in this Union a Republican Form of Government, and shall protect each of them against Invasion; and on Application of the Legislature, or of the Executive (when the Legislature cannot be convened) against domestic Violence.

ARTICLE V.

The Congress, whenever two-thirds of both Houses shall deem it necessary, shall propose Amendments to this Constitution, or, on the Application of the Legislatures of two-thirds of the several States, shall call a Convention for proposing Amendments, which, in either Case, shall be valid to all Intents and Purposes, as part of this Constitution, when ratified by the Legislatures of three-fourths of the several States, or by Conventions in three-fourths thereof, as the one or the other Mode of Ratification may be proposed by the Congress; *Provided* that no Amendment which may be made prior to the Year One thousand eight hundred and eight shall in any Manner affect the first and fourth Clauses in the Ninth Section of the first Article; and that no State, without its Consent, shall be deprived of its equal Suffrage in the Senate.

ARTICLE VI.

All Debts contracted and Engagements entered into, before the Adoption of this Constitution, shall be as valid against the United States under this Constitution, as under the Confederation. This Constitution, and the Laws of the United States which shall be made in Pursuance thereof; and all Treaties made, or which shall be made, under the Authority of the United States, shall be the supreme Law of the Land; and the Judges in every State shall be bound thereby, any Thing in the Constitution or Laws of any State to the Contrary notwithstanding.

The Senators and Representatives before mentioned, and the Members of the several State Legislatures, and all executive and judicial officers, both of the United States and of the several States, shall be bound by Oath or Affirmation to support this Constitution; but no religious Test shall ever be required as a qualification to any Office or public Trust under the United States.

ARTICLE VII.

The Ratification of the Conventions of nine States shall be sufficient for the Establishment of this Constitution between the States so ratifying the same.

done in Convention by the Unanimous Consent of the States present the Seventeenth Day of September in the Year of our Lord one thousand seven hundred and Eighty seven, and of the Independence of the United States of America the Twelfth. In Witness whereof We have hereunto subscribed our Names.

GEORGE WASHINGTON
President and deputy from Virginia

NEW HAMPSHIRE
John Langdon
Nicholas Gilman

PENNSYLVANIA
Benjamin Franklin
Thomas Mifflin
Robert Morris
George Clymer
Thomas FitzSimons
Jared Ingersoll
James Wilson
Gouverneur Morris

MASSACHUSETTS
Nathaniel Gorham
Rufus King

NEW YORK
Alexander Hamilton

NEW JERSEY
William Livingston
David Brearley
William Paterson
Jonathan Dayton

DELAWARE
George Read
Gunning Bedford, Jr.
John Dickinson
Richard Bassett
Jacob Broom

MARYLAND
James McHenry
Daniel of St. Thomas Jenifer
Daniel Carroll

CONNECTICUT
William Samuel Johnson
Roger Sherman

VIRGINIA
John Blair
James Madison, Jr.

NORTH CAROLINA
William Blount
Richard Dobbs Spaight
Hugh Williamson

SOUTH CAROLINA
John Rutledge
Charles Cotesworth Pinckney
Charles Pinckney
Pierce Butler

GEORGIA
William Few
Abraham Baldwin

ARTICLES IN ADDITION TO, AND AMENDMENT OF, THE CONSTITUTION OF THE UNITED STATES OF AMERICA, PROPOSED BY CONGRESS, AND RATIFIED BY THE LEGISLATURES OF THE SEVERAL STATES, PURSUANT TO THE FIFTH ARTICLE OF THE ORIGINAL CONSTITUTION

(ARTICLE I.)

Congress shall make no law respecting an establishment of religion, or prohibiting the free exercise thereof; or abridging the freedom of speech, or of the press; or the right of the people peaceably to assemble, and to petition the Government for a redress of grievances.

(ARTICLE II.)

A well regulated Militia, being necessary to the security of a free State, the right of the people to keep and bear Arms shall not be infringed.

(ARTICLE III.)

No Soldier, shall, in time of peace, be quartered in any house, without the consent of the Owner, nor in time of war, but in a manner to be prescribed by law.

(ARTICLE IV.)

The right of the people to be secure in their persons, houses, papers, and effects, against unreasonable searches and seizures, shall not be violated, and no Warrants shall issue, but upon probable cause, supported by Oath or affirmation, and particularly describing the place to be searched, and the persons or things to be seized.

(ARTICLE V.)

No person shall be held to answer for a capital or otherwise infamous crime, unless on a presentment or indictment of a Grand Jury, except in cases arising in the land or naval forces, or in the Militia, when in actual service in time of War or public danger; nor shall any person be subject for the same offence to be twice put in jeopardy of life or limb; nor shall be compelled in any criminal case to be a witness against himself, nor be deprived of life, liberty, or property, without due process of law; nor shall private property be taken for public use, without just compensation.

(ARTICLE VI.)

In all criminal prosecutions, the accused shall enjoy the right to a speedy and public trial, by an impartial jury of the State and district wherein the crime shall have been committed, which district shall have been previously ascertained by law, and to be informed of the nature and cause of the accusations; to be confronted with the witnesses against him; to have compulsory process for obtaining witnesses in his favor, and to have the Assistance of Counsel for his defence.

(ARTICLE VII.)

In suits at common law, where the value in controversy shall exceed twenty dollars, the right of trial by jury shall be preserved, and no fact tried by a jury, shall be otherwise reexamined in any Court of the United States, than according to the rules of the common law.

(ARTICLE VIII.)

Excessive bail shall not be required, nor excessive fines imposed, nor cruel and unusual punishments inflicted.

(ARTICLE IX.)

The enumeration in the Constitution, of certain rights, shall not be construed to deny or disparage others retained by the people.

(ARTICLE X.)

The powers not delegated to the United States by the Constitution, nor prohibited by it to the States, are reserved to the States respectively, or to the people.
(Amendments I–X, in force 1791.)

(ARTICLE XI.)

The Judicial power of the United States shall not be construed to extend to any suit in law or equity, commenced or prosecuted against one of the United States by Citizens of another State, or by Citizens or Subjects of any Foreign State.

(ARTICLE XII.)

The Electors shall meet in their respective States and vote by ballot for President and Vice-President, one of whom, at least, shall not be an inhabitant of the same State with themselves; they shall name in their ballots the person voted for as President, and in distinct ballots the person voted for as Vice-President, and they shall make distinct lists of all persons voted for as President, and of all persons voted for as Vice-President, and of the number of votes for each, which lists they shall sign and certify, and transmit sealed to the seat of the government of the United States, directed to the President of the Senate;—The President of the Senate shall, in the presence of the Senate and House of Representatives, open all the certificates and the votes shall then be counted;—The person having the greatest number of votes for President, shall be the President, if such number be a majority of the whole number of Electors appointed; and if no person have such majority, then from the persons having the highest numbers not exceeding three on the list of those voted for as President, the House of Representatives shall choose immediately, by ballot, the President. But in choosing the President, the votes shall be taken by states, the representation from each state having one vote; a quorum for this purpose shall consist of a member or members from two-thirds of the states, and a majority of all the states shall be necessary to a choice. And if the House of Representatives shall not choose a President whenever the right of choice shall devolve upon them, before the fourth day of March next following, then the Vice-President shall act as President, as in the case of the death or other constitutional disability of the President.—The person having the greatest number of votes as Vice-President, shall be the Vice-President, if such number be a majority of the whole number of Electors appointed, and if no person have a majority, then from the two highest numbers on the list, the Senate shall choose the Vice-President; a quorum for the purpose shall consist of two-thirds of the whole number of Senators, and a majority of the whole number shall be necessary to a choice. But no person constitutionally ineligible to the office of President shall be eligible to that of Vice-President of the United States.

(ARTICLE XIII.)

Section 1. Neither slavery nor involuntary servitude, except as a punishment for crime whereof the party shall have been duly convicted, shall exist within the United States, or any place subject to their jurisdiction.

Section 2. Congress shall have power to enforce this article by appropriate legislation.

(ARTICLE XIV.)

Section 1. All persons born or naturalized in the United States, and subject to the jurisdiction thereof, are citizens of the United States and of the State wherein they reside. No State shall make or enforce any law which shall abridge the privileges or immunities of citizens of the United States; nor shall any State deprive any person of life, liberty, or property, without due process of law; nor deny to any person within its jurisdiction the equal protection of the laws.

Section 2. Representatives shall be apportioned among the several States according to their respective numbers, counting the whole number of persons in each State, excluding Indians not taxed. But when the right to vote at any election for the choice of electors for President and Vice-President of the United States, Representatives in Congress, the Executive and Judicial officers of a State, or the members of the Legislature thereof, is denied to any of the male inhabitants of such State, being twenty-one years of age, and citizens of the United States, or in any way abridged, except for participation in rebellion, or other crime, the basis of representation therein shall be reduced in the proportion which the number of such male citizens shall bear to the whole number of male citizens twenty-one years of age in such State.

Section 3. No person shall be a Senator or Representative in Congress, or elector of President and Vice-President, or hold any office, civil or military, under the United States, or under any State, who, having previously taken an oath, as a member of Congress, or as an officer of the United States, or as a member of any State legislature, or as an executive or judicial officer of any State, to support the Constitution of the United States, shall have engaged in insurrection or rebellion against the same, or given aid or comfort to the enemies thereof. But Congress may by a vote of two-thirds of each House, remove such disability.

Section 4. The validity of the public debt of the United States, authorized by law, including debts incurred for payment of pensions and bounties for services in suppressing insurrection or rebellion, shall not be questioned. But neither the United States nor any State shall assume or pay any debt or obligation incurred in aid of insurrection or rebellion against the United States, or any claim for the loss or emancipation of any slave; but all such debts, obligations, and claims shall be held illegal and void.

Section 5. The Congress shall have the power to enforce, by appropriate legislation, the provisions of this article.

(ARTICLE XV.)

Section 1. The right of citizens of the United States to vote shall not be denied or abridged by the United States or by any State on account of race, color, or previous condition of servitude—

Section 2. The Congress shall have power to enforce this article by appropriate legislation.

(ARTICLE XVI.)

The Congress shall have power to lay and collect taxes on incomes, from whatever source derived, without apportionment among the several States, and without regard to any census or enumeration.

(ARTICLE XVII.)

The Senate of the United States shall be composed of two senators from each State, elected by the people thereof, for six years; and each senator shall have one vote. The electors in each State shall have the qualifications requisite for electors of the most numerous branch of the State legislature.

When vacancies happen in the representation of any State in the Senate, the executive authority of such State shall issue writs of election to fill such vacancies: *Provided,* That the legislature of any State may empower the executive thereof to make temporary appointments until the people fill the vacancies by election as the legislature may direct.

This amendment shall not be so construed as to affect the election or term of any Senator chosen before it becomes valid as part of the Constitution.

(ARTICLE XVIII.)

After one year from the ratification of this article, the manufacture, sale, or transportation of intoxicating liquors within, the importation thereof into, or the exportation thereof from the United States and all territory subject to the jurisdiction thereof for beverage purposes is hereby prohibited.

The Congress and the several States shall have concurrent power to enforce this article by appropriate legislation.

This article shall be inoperative unless it shall have been ratified as an amendment to the Constitution by the legislatures of the several States, as provided in the Constitution, within seven years from the date of the submission hereof to the States by the Congress.

(ARTICLE XIX.)

The right of citizens of the United States to vote shall not be denied or abridged by the United States or by any State on account of sex.

Congress shall have power to enforce this article by appropriate legislation.

(ARTICLE XX.)

Section 1. The terms of the President and Vice-President shall end at noon on the 20th day of January, and the terms of Senators and Representatives at noon on the 3d day of January, of the years in which such terms would have ended if this article had not been ratified; and the terms of their successors shall then begin.

Section 2. The Congress shall assemble at least once in every year, and such meeting shall begin at noon on the 3d day of January, unless they shall by law appoint a different day.

Section 3. If, at the time fixed for the beginning of the term of the President, the President elect shall have died, the Vice President elect shall become President. If a President shall not have been chosen before the time fixed for the beginning of his term, or if the President elect shall have failed to qualify, then the Vice President elect shall act as President until a President shall have qualified; and the Congress may by law provide for the case wherein neither a President elect nor a Vice President elect shall have qualified, declaring who shall then act as President, or the manner in which one who is to act shall be selected, and such person shall act accordingly until a President or Vice President shall have qualified.

Section 4. The Congress may by law provide for the case of the death of any of the persons from whom the House of Representatives may choose a President whenever the right of choice shall have devolved upon them, and for the case of the death of any of the persons from whom the Senate may choose a Vice President whenever the right of choice shall have devolved upon them.

Section 5. Sections 1 and 2 shall take effect on the 15th day of October following the ratification of this article.

Section 6. This article shall be inoperative unless it shall have been ratified as an amendment to the Constitution by the legislatures of three-fourths of the several States within seven years from the date of its submission.

(ARTICLE XXI.)

Section 1. The Eighteenth Article of amendment to the Constitution of the United States is hereby repealed.

Section 2. The transportation or importation into any State, Territory, or possession of the United States for delivery or use therein of intoxicating liquors in violation of the laws thereof, is hereby prohibited.

Section 3. This article shall be inoperative unless it shall have been ratified as an amendment to the Constitution by conventions in the several States, as provided in the Constitution, within seven years from the date of the submission thereof to the States by the Congress.

(ARTICLE XXII.)

No person shall be elected to the office of the President more than twice, and no person who has held the office of President, or acted as President for more than two years of a term to which some other person was elected President shall be elected to the office of the President more than once.

But this article shall not apply to any person holding the office of President when this article was proposed by the Congress, and shall not prevent any person who may be holding the office of President, or acting as President, during the term within which this article becomes operative from holding the office of President or acting as President during the remainder of such term.

This article shall be inoperative unless it shall have been ratified as an amendment to the Constitution by the legislatures of three-fourths of the several States within seven years from the date of its submission to the States by the Congress.

(ARTICLE XXIII.)

Section 1. Electors for the District of Columbia.—The District constituting the seat of Government of the United States shall appoint in such manner as the Congress may direct:

A number of electors of President and Vice President equal to the whole number of Senators and Representatives in Congress to which the district would be entitled if it were a State, but in no event more than the least populous State; they shall be in addition to those appointed by the States, but they shall be considered, for the purposes of the election of President and Vice President, to be electors appointed by a State; and they shall meet in the District and perform such duties as provided by the twelfth article of amendment.

Section 2. Enforcement.—The Congress shall have the power to enforce this article by appropriate legislation.

APPENDIX C

Presidential Elections, 1864–1960

YEAR	CANDIDATES	PARTIES	POPULAR VOTE	ELEC-TORAL VOTE
1864	ABRAHAM LINCOLN	Republican	2,213,655	212
	George B. McClellan	Democrat	1,805,237	21
1868	ULYSSES S. GRANT	Republican	3,012,833	214
	Horatio Seymour	Democrat	2,703,249	80
1872	ULYSSES S. GRANT	Republican	3,597,132	286
	Horace Greeley	Democrat-Liberal Republican	2,834,125	66
1876	RUTHERFORD B. HAYES	Republican	4,036,298	185
	Samuel J. Tilden	Democrat	4,300,590	184
1880	JAMES A. GARFIELD	Republican	4,454,416	214
	Winfield S. Hancock	Democrat	4,444,952	155
1884	GROVER CLEVELAND	Democrat	4,874,986	219
	James G. Blaine	Republican	4,851,981	182
1888	BENJAMIN HARRISON	Republican	5,439,853	233
	Grover Cleveland	Democrat	5,540,309	168
1892	GROVER CLEVELAND	Democrat	5,556,918	277
	Benjamin Harrison	Republican	5,176,108	145
	James B. Weaver	People's	1,041,028	22
1896	WILLIAM McKINLEY	Republican	7,104,779	271
	William J. Bryan	Democrat-People's	6,502,925	176
1900	WILLIAM McKINLEY	Republican	7,207,923	292
	William J. Bryan	Dem.-Populist	6,358,133	155
1904	THEODORE ROOSEVELT	Republican	7,623,486	336
	Alton B. Parker	Democrat	5,077,911	140
	Eugene V. Debs	Socialist	402,283	..
1908	WILLIAM H. TAFT	Republican	7,678,908	321
	William J. Bryan	Democrat	6,409,104	162
	Eugene V. Debs	Socialist	420,793	..
1912	WOODROW WILSON	Democrat	6,293,454	435
	William H. Taft	Republican	3,484,980	8
	Theodore Roosevelt	Progressive	4,119,538	88
	Eugene V. Debs	Socialist	900,672	..

YEAR	CANDIDATES	PARTIES	POPULAR VOTE	ELEC- TOTAL VOTE
1916	WOODROW WILSON	Democrat	9,129,606	277
	Charles E. Hughes	Republican	8,538,221	254
	A. L. Benson	Socialist	585,113	..
1920	WARREN G. HARDING	Republican	16,152,200	404
	James M. Cox	Democrat	9,147,353	127
	Eugene V. Debs	Socialist	919,799	..
1924	CALVIN COOLIDGE	Republican	15,725,016	382
	John W. Davis	Democrat	8,386,503	136
	Robert M. LaFollette	Progressive	4,822,856	13
1928	HERBERT HOOVER	Republican	21,391,381	444
	Alfred E. Smith	Democrat	15,016,443	87
	Norman Thomas	Socialist	267,835	..
1932	FRANKLIN D. ROOSEVELT	Democrat	22,821,857	472
	Herbert Hoover	Republican	15,761,841	59
	Norman Thomas	Socialist	881,951	..
1936	FRANKLIN D. ROOSEVELT	Democrat	27,751,597	523
	Alfred M. Landon	Republican	16,679,583	8
	William Lemke	Union & others	882,479	..
1940	FRANKLIN D. ROOSEVELT	Democrat	27,244,160	449
	Wendell L. Willkie	Republican	22,305,198	82
1944	FRANKLIN D. ROOSEVELT	Democrat	25,602,504	432
	Thomas E. Dewey	Republican	22,006,285	99
1948	HARRY S. TRUMAN	Democrat	24,105,695	303
	Thomas E. Dewey	Republican	21,969,170	189
	J. Strom Thurmond	State-Rights Democrat	1,169,021	39
	Henry A. Wallace	Progressive	1,156,103	..
1952	DWIGHT D. EISENHOWER	Republican	33,936,252	442
	Adlai E. Stevenson	Democrat	27,314,992	89
1956	DWIGHT D. EISENHOWER	Republican	35,575,420	457
	Adlai E. Stevenson	Democrat	26,033,066	74
1960	JOHN F. KENNEDY	Democrat	34,227,096	303
	Richard M. Nixon	Republican	34,107,646	219

APPENDIX D

Presidents and the Cabinets of the United States 1865–1961

PRESIDENT		TERM
ANDREW JOHNSON of Tennessee		1865–1869
Secretary of State	William H. Seward of N. Y.	1865–1869
Secretary of the Treasury	Hugh McCulloch of Ind.	1865–1869
Secretary of War	Edwin M. Stanton of Pa.	1865–1868
	John M. Schofield of Ill.	1868–1869
Attorney General	James Speed of Ky.	1865–1866
	Henry Stanbery of Ohio	1866–1868
	William M. Evarts of N. Y.	1868–1869
Postmaster General	William Dennison of Ohio	1865–1866
	Alexander W. Randall of Wis.	1866–1869
Secretary of the Navy	Gideon Welles of Conn.	1865–1869
Secretary of the Interior	James Harlan of Iowa	1865–1866
	Orville H. Browning of Ill.	1866–1869
ULYSSES S. GRANT of Illinois		1869–1877
Vice-President	Schuyler Colfax of Ind.	1869–1873
	Henry Wilson of Mass.	1873–1875
Secretary of State	Hamilton Fish of N. Y.	1869–1877
Secretary of the Treasury	George S. Boutwell of Mass.	1869–1873
	William A. Richardson of Mass.	1873–1874
	Benjamin H. Bristow of Ky.	1874–1876
	Lot M. Morrill of Me.	1876–1877
Secretary of War	John A. Rawlins of Ill.	1869
	William T. Sherman of Ohio	1869
	William W. Belknap of Iowa	1869–1876
	Alphonso Taft of Ohio	1876
	James D. Cameron of Pa.	1876–1877
Attorney General	Ebenezer R. Hoar of Mass.	1869–1870
	Amos T. Akerman of Ga.	1870–1871
	George H. Williams of Ore.	1872–1875
	Edwards Pierrepont of N. Y.	1875–1876
	Alphonso Taft of Ohio	1876–1877
Postmaster General	John A. J. Creswell of Md.	1869–1874
	James W. Marshall of Va.	1874
	Marshall Jewell of Conn.	1874–1876
	James N. Tyner of Ind.	1876–1877

PRESIDENT		TERM
Secretary of the Navy	Adolph E. Borie of Pa.	1869
	George M. Robeson of N. J.	1869–1877
Secretary of the Interior	Jacob D. Cox of Ohio	1869–1870
	Columbus Delano of Ohio	1870–1875
	Zachariah Chandler of Mich.	1875–1877
RUTHERFORD B. HAYES of Ohio		1877–1881
Vice-President	William A. Wheeler of N. Y.	1877–1881
Secretary of State	William M. Evarts of N. Y.	1877–1881
Secretary of the Treasury	John Sherman of Ohio	1877–1881
Secretary of War	George W. McCrary of Iowa	1877–1879
	Alexander Ramsey of Minn.	1879–1881
Attorney General	Charles Devens of Mass.	1877–1881
Postmaster General	David M. Key of Tenn.	1877–1880
	Horace Maynard of Tenn.	1880–1881
Secretary of the Navy	Richard W. Thompson of Ind.	1877–1880
	Nathan Goff, Jr. of W. Va.	1881
Secretary of the Interior	Carl Schurz of Mo.	1877–1881
JAMES A. GARFIELD of Ohio		1881
Vice-President	Chester A. Arthur of N. Y.	1881
Secretary of State	James G. Blaine of Me.	1881
Secretary of the Treasury	William Windom of Minn.	1881
Secretary of War	Robert T. Lincoln of Ill.	1881
Attorney General	Wayne MacVeagh of Pa.	1881
Postmaster General	Thomas L. James of N. Y.	1881
Secretary of the Navy	William H. Hunt of La.	1881
Secretary of the Interior	Samuel J. Kirkwood of Iowa	1881
CHESTER A. ARTHUR of New York		1881–1885
Secretary of State	Frederick T. Frelinghuysen of N. J.	1881–1885
Secretary of the Treasury	Charles J. Folger of N. Y.	1881–1884
	Hugh McCulloch of Ind.	1884–1885
Secretary of War	Robert T. Lincoln of Ill.	1881–1885
Attorney General	Benjamin H. Brewster of Pa.	1882–1885
Postmaster General	Thomas L. James of N. Y.	1881
	Timothy O. Howe of Wis.	1882–1883
	Walter Q. Gresham of Ind.	1883–1884
	Frank Hatton of Iowa	1884–1885
Secretary of the Navy	William E. Chandler of N. H.	1882–1885
Secretary of the Interior	Samuel J. Kirkwood of Iowa	1881
	Henry M. Teller of Colo.	1882–1885

PRESIDENT		TERM
GROVER CLEVELAND of New York		1885–1889
Vice-President	Thomas J. Hendricks of Ind.	1885
Secretary of State	Thomas F. Bayard of Del.	1885–1889
Secretary of the Treasury	Daniel Manning of N. Y.	1885–1887
	Charles S. Fairchild of N. Y.	1887–1889
Secretary of War	William C. Endicott of Mass.	1885–1889
Attorney General	Augustus H. Garland of Ark.	1885–1889
Postmaster General	William F. Vilas of Wis.	1885–1888
	Don M. Dickinson of Mich.	1888–1889
Secretary of the Navy	William C. Whitney of N. Y.	1885–1889
Secretary of the Interior	Lucius Q. C. Lamar of Miss.	1885–1888
	William F. Vilas of Wis.	1888–1889
Secretary of Agriculture	Norman J. Colman of Mo.	1889
BENJAMIN HARRISON of Indiana		1889–1893
Vice-President	Levi P. Morton of N. Y.	1889–1893
Secretary of State	James G. Blaine of Me.	1889–1892
	John W. Foster of Ind.	1892–1893
Secretary of the Treasury	William Windom of Minn.	1889–1891
	Charles Foster of Ohio	1891–1893
Secretary of War	Redfield Proctor of Vt.	1889–1891
	Stephen B. Elkins of W. Va.	1891–1893
Attorney General	William H. H. Miller of Ind.	1889–1893
Postmaster General	John Wanamaker of Pa.	1889–1893
Secretary of the Navy	Benjamin F. Tracy of N. Y.	1889–1893
Secretary of the Interior	John W. Noble of Mo.	1889–1893
Secretary of Agriculture	Jeremiah M. Rusk of Wis.	1889–1893
GROVER CLEVELAND of New York		1893–1897
Vice-President	Adlai E. Stevenson of Ill.	1893–1897
Secretary of State	Walter Q. Gresham of Ill.	1893–1895
	Richard Olney of Mass.	1895–1897
Secretary of the Treasury	John G. Carlisle of Ky.	1893–1897
Secretary of War	Daniel S. Lamont of N. Y.	1893–1897
Attorney General	Richard Olney of Mass.	1893–1895
	Judson Harmon of Ohio	1895–1897
Postmaster General	Wilson S. Bissell of N. Y.	1893–1895
	William L. Wilson of W. Va.	1895–1897
Secretary of the Navy	Hilary A. Herbert of Ala.	1893–1897
Secretary of the Interior	Hoke Smith of Ga.	1893–1896
	David R. Francis of Mo.	1896–1897
Secretary of Agriculture	Julius Sterling Morton of Neb.	1893–1897

PRESIDENT		TERM
WILLIAM McKINLEY of Ohio		1897–1901
Vice-President	Garrett A. Hobert of N. J.	1897–1899
	Theodore Roosevelt of N. Y.	1901
Secretary of State	John Sherman of Ohio	1897–1898
	William R. Day of Ohio	1898
	John Hay of D.C.	1898–1901
Secretary of the Treasury	Lyman J. Gage of Ill.	1897–1901
Secretary of War	Russell A. Alger of Mich.	1897–1899
	Elihu Root of N. Y.	1899–1901
Attorney General	Joseph McKenna of Cal.	1897–1898
	John W. Griggs of N. J.	1898–1901
	Philander C. Knox of Pa.	1901
Postmaster General	James A. Gary of Md.	1897–1898
	Charles Emory Smith of Pa.	1898–1901
Secretary of the Navy	John D. Long of Mass.	1897–1901
Secretary of the Interior	Cornelius N. Bliss of N. Y.	1897–1898
	Ethan A. Hitchcock of Mo.	1898–1901
Secretary of Agriculture	James Wilson of Iowa	1897–1901
THEODORE ROOSEVELT of New York		1901–1909
Vice-President	Charles Warren Fairbanks of Ind.	1905–1909
Secretary of State	John Hay of D.C.	1901–1905
	Elihu Root of N. Y.	1905–1909
	Robert Bacon of N. Y.	1909
Secretary of the Treasury	Lyman J. Gage of Ill.	1901–1902
	Leslie M. Shaw of Iowa	1902–1907
	George B. Cortelyou of N. Y.	1907–1909
Secretary of War	Elihu Root of N. Y.	1901–1904
	William H. Taft of Ohio	1904–1908
	Luke E. Wright of Tenn.	1908–1909
Attorney General	Philander C. Knox of Pa.	1901–1904
	William H. Moody of Mass.	1904–1906
	Charles J. Bonaparte of Md.	1906–1909
Postmaster General	Charles Emory Smith of Pa.	1901–1902
	Henry C. Payne of Wis.	1902–1904
	Robert J. Wynne of Pa.	1904–1905
	George B. Cortelyou of N. Y.	1905–1907
	George von L. Meyer of Mass.	1907–1909
Secretary of the Navy	John D. Long of Mass.	1901–1902
	William H. Moody of Mass.	1902–1904
	Paul Morton of Ill.	1904–1905
	Charles Bonaparte of Md.	1905–1906
	Victor H. Metcalf of Cal.	1906–1908
	Truman H. Newberry of Mich.	1908–1909

PRESIDENT		TERM
Secretary of the Interior	Ethan A. Hitchcock of Mo.	1901–1907
	James R. Garfield of Ohio	1907–1909
Secretary of Agriculture	James Wilson of Iowa	1901–1909
Secretary of Commerce and Labor	George B. Cortelyou of N. Y.	1903–1904
	Victor H. Metcalf of Cal.	1904–1906
	Oscar S. Straus of N. Y.	1906–1909
WILLIAM H. TAFT of Ohio		1909–1913
Vice-President	James S. Sherman of N. Y.	1909–1912
Secretary of State	Philander C. Knox of Pa.	1909–1913
Secretary of the Treasury	Franklin MacVeagh of Ill.	1909–1913
Secretary of War	Jacob M. Dickinson of Tenn.	1909–1911
	Henry L. Stimson of N. Y.	1911–1913
Attorney General	George W. Wickersham of N. Y.	1909–1913
Postmaster General	Frank H. Hitchcock of Mass.	1909–1913
Secretary of the Navy	George von L. Meyer of Mass.	1909–1913
Secretary of the Interior	Richard A. Ballinger of Wash.	1909–1911
	Walter L. Fisher of Ill.	1911–1913
Secretary of Agriculture	James Wilson of Iowa	1909–1913
Secretary of Commerce and Labor	Charles Nagel of Mo.	1909–1913
WOODROW WILSON of New Jersey		1913–1921
Vice-President	Thomas R. Marshall of Ind.	1913–1921
Secretary of State	William Jennings Bryan of Neb.	1913–1915
	Robert Lansing of N. Y.	1915–1920
	Bainbridge Colby of N. Y.	1920–1921
Secretary of the Treasury	William Gibbs McAdoo of N. Y.	1913–1918
	Carter Glass of Va.	1918–1920
	David F. Houston of Mo.	1920–1921
Secretary of War	Lindley M. Garrison of N. J.	1913–1916
	Newton D. Baker of Ohio	1916–1921
Attorney General	James C. McReynolds of Tenn.	1913–1914
	Thomas W. Gregory of Texas	1914–1919
	A. Mitchell Palmer of Pa.	1919–1921
Postmaster General	Albert Sidney Burleson of Texas	1913–1921
Secretary of the Navy	Josephus Daniels of N. C.	1913–1921
Secretary of the Interior	Franklin K. Lane of Cal.	1913–1920
	John Barton Payne of Ill.	1920–1921
Secretary of Agriculture	David F. Houston of Mo.	1913–1920
	Edwin T. Meredith of Iowa	1920–1921
Secretary of Commerce	William C. Redfield of N. Y.	1913–1919
	Joshua W. Alexander of Mo.	1919–1921
Secretary of Labor	William B. Wilson of Pa.	1913–1921

PRESIDENT		TERM
WARREN G. HARDING of Ohio		1921–1923
Vice-President	Calvin Coolidge of Mass.	1921–1923
Secretary of State	Charles Evans Hughes of N. Y.	1921–1923
Secretary of the Treasury	Andrew W. Mellon of Pa.	1921–1923
Secretary of War	John W. Weeks of Mass.	1921–1923
Attorney General	Harry M. Daugherty of Ohio	1921–1923
Postmaster General	Will H. Hays of Ind.	1921–1922
	Hubert Work of Colo.	1922–1923
	Harry S. New of Ind.	1923
Secretary of the Navy	Edwin Denby of Mich.	1921–1923
Secretary of the Interior	Albert B. Fall of N. M.	1921–1923
	Hubert Work of Colo.	1923
Secretary of Agriculture	Henry C. Wallace of Iowa	1921–1923
Secretary of Commerce	Herbert C. Hoover of Cal.	1921–1923
Secretary of Labor	James J. Davis of Pa.	1921–1923
CALVIN COOLIDGE of Massachusetts		1923–1929
Vice-President	Charles G. Dawes of Ill.	1925–1929
Secretary of State	Charles Evans Hughes of N. Y.	1923–1925
	Frank B. Kellogg of Minn.	1925–1929
Secretary of the Treasury	Andrew W. Mellon of Pa.	1923–1929
Secretary of War	John W. Weeks of Mass.	1923–1925
	Dwight F. Davis of Mo.	1925–1929
Attorney General	Harry M. Daugherty of Ohio	1923–1924
	Harlan F. Stone of N. Y.	1924–1925
	John G. Sargent of Vt.	1925–1929
Postmaster General	Harry S. New of Ind.	1925–1929
Secretary of the Navy	Edwin Denby of Mich.	1923–1924
	Curtis D. Wilbur of Cal.	1924–1929
Secretary of the Interior	Hubert Work of Colo.	1923–1928
	Roy O. West of Ill.	1928–1929
Secretary of Agriculture	Henry C. Wallace of Iowa	1923–1924
	Howard M. Gore of W. Va.	1924–1925
	William M. Jardine of Kan.	1925–1929
Secretary of Commerce	Herbert C. Hoover of Cal.	1923–1928
	William F. Whiting of Mass.	1928–1929
Secretary of Labor	James J. Davis of Pa.	1923–1929
HERBERT C. HOOVER of California		1929–1933
Vice-President	Charles Curtis of Kan.	1929–1933
Secretary of State	Henry L. Stimson of N. Y.	1929–1933
Secretary of the Treasury	Andrew W. Mellon of Pa.	1929–1932
	Ogden L. Mills of N. Y.	1932–1933

PRESIDENT		TERM
Secretary of War	James W. Good of Ill.	1929
	Patrick J. Hurley of Okla.	1929–1933
Attorney General	James D. Mitchell of Minn.	1929–1933
Postmaster General	Walter F. Brown of Ohio	1929–1933
Secretary of the Navy	Charles F. Adams of Mass.	1929–1933
Secretary of the Interior	Ray L. Wilbur of Cal.	1929–1933
Secretary of Agriculture	Arthur M. Hyde of Mo.	1929–1933
Secretary of Commerce	Robert P. Lamont of Ill.	1929–1932
	Roy D. Chapin of Mich.	1932–1933
Secretary of Labor	James J. Davis of Pa.	1929–1930
	William N. Doak of Va.	1930–1933
FRANKLIN DELANO ROOSEVELT of New York		1933–1945
Vice-President	John N. Garner of Texas	1933–1941
	Henry A. Wallace of Iowa	1941–1945
	Harry S. Truman of Mo.	1945
Secretary of State	Cordell Hull of Tenn.	1933–1944
	Edward R. Stettinius of Va.	1944–1945
Secretary of the Treasury	William H. Woodin of N. Y.	1933–1934
	Henry Morgenthau, Jr. of N. Y.	1934–1945
Secretary of War	George H. Dern of Utah	1933–1936
	Harry H. Woodring of Kan.	1936–1940
	Henry L. Stimson of N. Y.	1940–1945
Attorney General	Homer S. Cummings of Conn.	1933–1939
	Frank Murphy of Mich.	1939–1940
	Robert H. Jackson of N. Y.	1940–1941
	Francis Biddle of Pa.	1941–1945
Postmaster General	James A. Farley of N. Y.	1933–1940
	Frank C. Walker of Pa.	1940–1945
Secretary of the Navy	Claude A. Swanson of Va.	1933–1939
	Charles Edison of N. J.	1939–1940
	Frank Knox of Ill.	1940–1944
	James V. Forrestal of N. Y.	1944–1945
Secretary of the Interior	Harold L. Ickes of Ill.	1933–1945
Secretary of Agriculture	Henry A. Wallace of Iowa	1933–1940
	Claude R. Wickard of Ind.	1940–1945
Secretary of Commerce	Daniel C. Roper of S. C.	1933–1938
	Harry L. Hopkins of N. Y.	1938–1940
	Jesse H. Jones of Texas	1940–1945
	Henry A. Wallace of Iowa	1945
Secretary of Labor	Frances Perkins of N. Y.	1933–1945

PRESIDENT		TERM
HARRY S. TRUMAN of Missouri		1945–1953
Vice-President	Alben W. Barkley of Ky.	1949–1953
Secretary of State	Edward R. Stettinius of Va.	1945
	James F. Byrnes of S. C.	1945–1947
	George C. Marshall of Pa.	1947–1949
	Dean G. Acheson of Conn.	1949–1953
Secretary of the Treasury	Fred M. Vinson of Ky.	1945–1946
	John W. Snyder of Mo.	1946–1953
Secretary of Defense	James V. Forrestal of N. Y.	1947–1949
	Louis A. Johnson of W. Va.	1949–1953
Secretary of War	Robert P. Patterson of N. Y.	1945–1947
	Kenneth C. Royall of N. C.	1947
Attorney General	Francis Biddle of Pa.	1945
	Tom C. Clark of Texas	1945–1949
	J. Howard McGrath of R. I.	1949–1953
Postmaster General	Frank C. Walker of Pa.	1945
	Robert E. Hannegan of Mo.	1945–1947
	Jesse M. Donaldson of Mo.	1947–1953
Secretary of the Navy	James V. Forrestal of N. Y.	1945–1947
Secretary of the Interior	Harold L. Ickes of Ill.	1945–1946
	Julius A. Krug of Wis.	1946–1949
	Oscar L. Chapman of Col.	1949–1953
Secretary of Agriculture	Claude R. Wickard of Ind.	1945
	Clinton P. Anderson of N. M.	1945–1948
	Charles F. Brannan of Colo.	1948–1953
Secretary of Commerce	Henry A. Wallace of Iowa	1945–1946
	William Averell Harriman of N. Y.	1946–1948
	Charles Sawyer of Ohio	1948–1953
Secretary of Labor	Frances Perkins of N. Y.	1945
	Lewis B. Schwellenbach of Wash.	1945–1948
	Maurice J. Tobin of Mass.	1948–1953
DWIGHT D. EISENHOWER of Pennsylvania		1953–1961
Vice-President	Richard M. Nixon of Cal.	1953–1961
Secretary of State	John Foster Dulles of N. Y.	1953–1959
	Christian A. Herter of Mass.	1959–1961
Secretary of the Treasury	George M. Humphrey of Ohio	1953–1957
	Robert B. Anderson of Tex.	1957–1961
Secretary of Defense	Charles E. Wilson of Mich.	1953–1957
	Neil H. McElroy of Ohio	1957–1959
	Thomas S. Gates, Jr. of Pa.	1959–1961
Attorney General	Herbert Brownell, Jr. of N. Y.	1953–1957
	William P. Rogers of N. Y.	1957–1961

Postmaster General	A. E. Summerfield of Mich.	1953–1961
Secretary of the Interior	Douglas McKay of Ore.	1953–1956
	Fred A. Seaton of Neb.	1956–1961
Secretary of Agriculture	Ezra Taft Benson of Utah	1953–1961
Secretary of Commerce	Sinclair Weeks of Mass.	1953–1958
	Lewis L. Strauss	1958
	Frederick H. Mueller	1959–1961
Secretary of Labor	Martin P. Durkin of Ill.	1953
	James P. Mitchell of N. J.	1953–1961
Secretary of Health, Education, and Welfare	Oveta Culp Hobby of Texas	1953–1955
	Marion B. Folsom of N. Y.	1955–1958
	Arthur S. Flemming of Ohio	1958–1961

JOHN F. KENNEDY of Massachusetts 1961–

Vice-President	Lyndon B. Johnson of Tex.	1961–
Secretary of State	Dean Rusk	1961–
Secretary of the Treasury	C. Douglas Dillon	1961–
Secretary of Defense	Robert S. McNamara	1961–
Attorney General	Robert F. Kennedy	1961–
Postmaster General	J. Edward Day	1961–
Secretary of the Interior	Stewart L. Udall	1961–
Secretary of Agriculture	Orville L. Freeman	1961–
Secretary of Commerce	Luther H. Hodges	1961–
Secretary of Labor	Arthur J. Goldberg	1961–
Secretary of Health, Education, and Welfare	Abraham A. Ribicoff	1961–

APPENDIX E

Chronological Chart

1867	Alaska purchased from Russia.
1868	President Johnson acquitted.
1868	"Erie War," an example of stock manipulation of this period.
1869	First transcontinental railroad completed.
1869	Knights of Labor founded.
1873	Panic of 1873
1877	Radical Reconstruction ended in the South.
1878	Bland-Allison Act passed.
1879	Rockefeller formed Standard Oil trust.
1881	Edison invented incandescent light.
1881	Formation of A. F. of L.
1881	Garfield assassinated: Arthur becomes President.
1882	Chinese Exclusion Act.
1883	Pendleton Act passed.
1886	Radicals and police clashed in Haymarket Massacre.
1887	Interstate Commerce Act passed.
1890	Sherman Anti-Trust Act passed.
1890	Sherman Silver Purchase Act passed.
1890	1890 Census stated that the frontier no longer existed.
1889–90	Six Western states admitted.
1893	Sherman Silver Purchase Act repealed.
1893–96	Panic of 1893.
1894	Pullman strike.
1898	Spanish-American War (April 21–December 10).
1898	Hawaii annexed.
1899	Open Door policy for China.
1901	McKinley assassinated; Theodore Roosevelt became President.
1903	U. S. secured rights to Panama Canal route.
1906	Hepburn Act passed.
1906	Great earthquake destroyed San Francisco.
1907–8	Panic of 1907.
1910	Mann-Elkins Act (interstate commerce) passed.
1912	Teddy Roosevelt ran as Progressive against Taft.
1913	Federal Reserve System established.
1914	Federal Trade Commission established.
1914	Panama Canal opened.
1914	World War I began in Europe.
1915	"Lusitania" sunk.
1917	U. S. declared war on Germany, April 6.
1917	U. S. purchased Virgin Islands from Denmark.
1918	Armistice signed, November 11.
1919	Prohibition Amendment ratified.
1919	Treaty of Versailles signed in Paris, June 28.
1920	Women's suffrage provided by 19th Amendment.
1920	First regular radio broadcasting begun in Pittsburgh.
1921–22	Washington Naval Conference held.
1924	"Teapot Dome" scandals exposed in Congress.
1925	Famous "Scopes Trial" in Dayton, Tennessee.
1927	Sacco and Vanzetti executed.
1929	Federal Farm Board established.
1929	Crash of 1929.
1930	Hawley-Smoot Tariff Act.
1932	Reconstruction Finance Corporation established.
1933	"Hundred Days" of New Deal legislation created National Industrial Recovery Act (NIRA), Agricultural Adjustment Act (AAA), Civilian Conservation Corps (CCC), Tennessee Valley Authority (TVA), and other acts.

1935 Works Projects Administration created, April 8.

1935 C.I.O. split from A. F. of L.

1936 Supreme Court declared AAA unconstitutional.

1937 Supreme Court declared Wagner Act constitutional.

1937 1937 Recession.

1938 Second Agricultural Adjustment Act passed.

1939 German attack on Poland began World War II, September 1.

1940 France surrendered to Germany, June 22.

1941 Lend-Lease enacted, March 11.

1941 Atlantic Charter proclaimed, August 14.

1941 Pearl Harbor attacked by Japanese, December 7.

1943 Italy surrendered.

1943 Teheran Conference.

1944 D-Day (Normandy invasion), June 6.

1945 Yalta Conference.

1945 President Roosevelt died, April 12.

1945 First A-bomb detonated at Alamogordo, N. M., July 16.

1945 San Francisco UN Conference, April 25–June 26.

1945 V–E Day (German surrender), May 8.

1945 Potsdam Conference.

1945 Hiroshima hit by atomic bomb, August 6.

1945 V–J Day (Japanese surrender), August 15.

1948 Marshall Plan approved by Congress, April 3.

1949 Truman proposed "Fair Deal" program, January 5.

1950 Korean War broke out, June 25.

1953 First hydrogen bomb exploded in Pacific, February 2.

1953 Dept. of Health, Education, and Welfare created, April 1.

1954 "Nautilus," first nuclear submarine, launched, January 21.

1954 Supreme Court banned school segregation, May 17.

1955 Salk Polio vaccine proved effective, April 12.

1956 Hungarian revolt.

1956 Suez crisis.

1957 Eisenhower Doctrine announced, January 5.

1957 First civil rights bill since 1870's enacted, August 29.

1957 Little Rock segregation crisis erupted, September.

1957 First Soviet Sputnik fired into orbit, October 4.

1958 First U. S. earth satellite orbited, January 31.

APPENDIX F

Major American Political Parties, 1864–1960

	UNION and DEM.				
1864	Johnson (1865–69)				
	REPUBLICAN				**PROHIBITION**
1868	Grant (1869–77)				
		LIB. REPUB.		**ANTI-MONOPOLY**	
1872		Greeley		**GRANGER**	
				GREENBACK	
1876	Hayes (1877–81)				
1880	Garfield (1881) Arthur (1881–85)				
			DEMOCRATIC		
1884			Cleveland (1885–89)		
1888	Harrison (1889–93)				
				POPULIST	**SOCIAL.-LABOR**
1892			Cleveland (1893–97)		
1896	McKinley (1897–1901)				
					SOCIALIST
1900	McKinley Roosevelt (1901–09)				
1904					
1908	Taft (1909–13)				
		PROGRESSIVE			
1912		Roosevelt	Wilson (1913–21)		
1916					
					COMMUNIST (Workers)
1920	Harding (1921–23) Coolidge (1923–29)				
1924		LaFollette			
1928	Hoover (1929–33)				
1932			Roosevelt (1933–45)		
1944			Roosevelt Truman (1945–53)		
1948		Wallace			
1952	Eisenhower (1953–61)				
1960			Kennedy (1961–)		

APPENDIX G

Speakers of the House of Representatives 1865–1962

Schuyler Colfax of Indiana	1863–1869
James G. Blaine of Maine	1869–1875
Michael C. Kerr of Indiana	1875–1876
Samuel J. Randall of Pennsylvania	1876–1881
Joseph W. Keifer of Ohio	1881–1883
John G. Carlisle of Kentucky	1883–1889
Thomas B. Reed of Maine	1889–1891
Charles F. Crisp of Georgia	1891–1895
Thomas B. Reed of Maine	1895–1899
David B. Henderson of Iowa	1899–1903
Joseph G. Cannon of Illinois	1903–1910
Champ Clark of Missouri	1911–1919
Frederick H. Gillet of Massachusetts	1919–1925
Nicholas Longworth of Ohio	1925–1931
John Nance Garner of Texas	1931–1933
Henry T. Rainey of Illinois	1933–1934
Joseph W. Byrns of Tennessee	1935–1936
William B. Bankhead of Alabama	1936–1940
Sam Rayburn of Texas	1940–1947
Joseph W. Martin, Jr. of Massachusetts	1947–1949
Sam Rayburn of Texas	1949–1953
Joseph W. Martin, Jr. of Massachusetts	1953–1955
Sam Rayburn of Texas	1955–1961
John W. McCormack of Massachusetts	1962–

APPENDIX H

Justices of the United States Supreme Court 1865–1959

Name	
Salmon P. Chase of Ohio (Chief Justice)	1864–1873
James M. Wayne of Ga.	1835–1867
Samuel Nelson of N. Y.	1845–1872
Robert C. Grier of Pa.	1846–1870
Nathan Clifford of Me.	1858–1881
Noah H. Swayne of Ohio	1862–1881
Samuel F. Miller of Iowa	1862–1890
David Davis of Ill.	1862–1877
Stephen J. Field of Cal.	1863–1897
William Strong of Pa.	1870–1880
Joseph P. Bradley of N. J.	1870–1892
Ward Hunt of N. Y.	1873–1882
Morrison R. Waite of Ohio (Chief Justice	1874–1888
John M. Harlan of Ky.	1877–1911
William B. Woods of Ga.	1881–1887
Stanley Matthews of Ohio	1881–1889
Horace Gray of Mass.	1882–1902
Samuel Blatchford of N. Y.	1882–1893
Lucius Q. C. Lamar of Miss.	1888–1893
Melville W. Fuller of Ill. (Chief Justice)	1888–1910
David J. Brewer of Kan.	1890–1910
Henry B. Brown of Mich.	1891–1906
George Shiras, Jr. of Pa.	1892–1903
Howell E. Jackson of Tenn.	1893–1895
Edward D. White of La.	1894–1910
Rufus W. Peckham of N. Y.	1896–1909
Joseph McKenna of Cal.	1898–1925
Oliver W. Holmes of Mass.	1902–1932
William R. Day of Ohio	1903–1922
William H. Moody of Mass.	1906–1910
Horace H. Lurton of Tenn.	1910–1914
Charles E. Hughes of N. Y.	1910–1916
Willis Van Devanter of Wy.	1911–1937
Joseph R. Lamar of Ga.	1911–1916
Edward D. White of La. (Chief Justice)	1910–1921

Mahlon Pitney of N. J.	1912–1922
James C. McReynolds of Tenn.	1914–1941
Louis D. Brandeis of Mass.	1916–1939
John H. Clarke of Ohio	1916–1922
William H. Taft of Conn. (Chief Justice)	1921–1930
George Sutherland of Utah	1922–1938
Pierce Butler of Minn.	1922–1939
Edward T. Sanford of Tenn.	1923–1930
Harlan F. Stone of N. Y.	1925–1941
Charles E. Hughes of N. Y. (Chief Justice)	1930–1941
Owen J. Roberts of Pa.	1930–1945
Benjamin N. Cardozo of N. Y.	1932–1938
Hugo L. Black of Ala.	1937–
Stanley F. Reed of Ky.	1938–1957
Felix Frankfurter of Mass.	1939–
William O. Douglas of Conn.	1939–
Frank Murphy of Michigan	1940–1949
Harlan F. Stone of N. Y. (Chief Justice)	1941–1946
James F. Byrnes of S. C.	1941–1942
Robert H. Jackson of N. Y.	1941–1954
Wiley B. Rutledge of Iowa	1943–1949
Harold H. Burton of Ohio	1945–1958
Fred M. Vinson of Kentucky (Chief Justice)	1946–1953
Tom C. Clark of Texas	1949–
Sherman Minton of Ind.	1949–1956
Earl Warren of Calif. (Chief Justice)	1953–
John Marshall Harlan of N. Y.	1955–
William J. Brennan Jr., of N. J.	1956–
Charles E. Whittaker of Mo.	1957–
Potter Stewart of Ohio	1958–

APPENDIX I

The Admission of States to the Union 1865–1959

	DATE OF ADMISSION	AREA IN SQUARE MILES
Nebraska	Mar. 1, 1867	76,612
Colorado	Aug. 1, 1876	103,884
North Dakota	Nov. 2, 1889	69,457
South Dakota	Nov. 2, 1889	76,378
Montana	Nov. 8, 1889	145,736
Washington	Nov. 11, 1889	66,709
Idaho	July 3, 1890	82,708
Wyoming	July 10, 1890	97,411
Utah	Jan. 4, 1896	82,339
Oklahoma	Nov. 16, 1907	68,887
New Mexico	Jan. 6, 1912	121,510
Arizona	Feb. 14, 1912	113,525
Alaska	Jan. 3, 1959	586,400
Hawaii	Aug. 21, 1959	6,415

APPENDIX J

The Population of the United States, 1870–1960[1]

	1870	1880	1890	1900	1910	1920	1930	1940	1950	1960
Alabama	996,992	1,262,505	1,513,401	1,828,697	2,138,093	2,348,174	2,646,248	2,832,961	3,061,743	3,266,740
Alaska	....	....	....	....	....	....	....	....	....	226,167
Arizona	9,658	40,440	88,243	122,931	204,354	334,162	435,573	499,261	749,587	1,302,161
Arkansas	484,471	802,525	1,128,211	1,311,564	1,574,449	1,752,204	1,854,482	1,949,387	1,909,511	1,786,272
California	560,247	864,694	1,213,398	1,485,053	2,377,549	3,426,861	5,677,251	6,907,387	10,586,223	15,717,204
Colorado	39,864	194,327	413,249	539,700	799,024	939,629	1,035,791	1,123,296	1,325,089	1,753,947
Connecticut	537,454	622,700	746,258	908,420	1,114,756	1,380,631	1,606,903	1,709,242	2,007,280	2,535,234
Delaware	125,015	146,608	168,493	184,735	202,322	223,003	238,380	266,505	318,085	446,292
District of Columbia	131,700	177,624	230,392	278,718	331,069	437,571	486,869	663,091	802,178	763,956
Florida	187,748	269,493	391,422	528,542	752,619	968,470	1,468,211	1,897,414	2,771,305	4,951,560
Georgia	1,184,109	1,542,180	1,837,353	2,216,331	2,609,121	2,895,832	2,908,506	3,123,723	3,444,578	3,943,116
Hawaii	....	....	....	....	....	....	....	....	....	632,772
Idaho	14,999	32,610	88,548	161,772	325,594	431,866	445,032	524,873	586,637	667,191
Illinois	2,539,891	3,077,871	3,826,352	4,821,550	5,638,591	6,485,280	7,630,654	7,897,241	8,712,176	10,081,158
Indiana	1,680,637	1,978,301	2,192,404	2,516,462	2,700,876	2,930,390	3,238,503	3,427,796	3,934,224	4,662,498
Iowa	1,194,020	1,624,615	1,912,297	2,231,853	2,224,771	2,404,021	2,470,939	2,538,268	2,621,073	2,757,537
Kansas	364,399	996,096	1,428,108	1,470,495	1,690,949	1,769,257	1,880,999	1,801,028	1,905,299	2,178,611
Kentucky	1,321,011	1,648,690	1,858,635	2,147,174	2,289,905	2,416,630	2,614,589	2,845,627	2,944,806	3,038,156
Louisiana	726,915	939,946	1,118,588	1,381,625	1,656,388	1,798,509	2,101,593	2,363,880	2,683,516	3,257,022
Maine	626,915	648,936	661,086	694,466	742,371	768,014	797,423	847,226	969,265	913,774
Maryland	780,894	934,943	1,042,390	1,188,044	1,295,346	1,449,661	1,631,526	1,821,244	2,343,001	3,100,689
Massachusetts	1,457,351	1,783,085	2,238,947	2,805,346	3,366,416	3,852,356	4,249,614	4,316,721	4,690,514	5,148,578
Michigan	1,184,059	1,636,937	2,093,890	2,420,982	2,840,173	3,668,412	4,842,325	5,256,106	6,371,766	7,823,194
Minnesota	439,706	780,773	1,310,283	1,751,394	2,075,708	2,387,125	2,563,953	2,792,300	2,982,483	3,413,864
Mississippi	827,922	1,131,597	1,289,600	1,551,270	1,797,114	1,790,618	2,009,821	2,183,796	2,178,914	2,178,141
Missouri	1,721,295	2,168,380	2,679,185	3,106,665	3,293,335	3,404,055	3,629,367	3,784,664	3,954,653	4,319,813
Montana	20,595	39,159	142,924	243,329	376,053	548,889	537,606	559,456	591,024	674,767
Nebraska	122,993	452,402	1,062,656	1,066,300	1,192,214	1,296,372	1,377,963	1,315,834	1,325,510	1,411,330
Nevada	42,491	62,266	47,355	42,335	81,875	77,407	91,058	110,247	160,083	285,278
New Hampshire	318,300	346,991	376,530	411,588	430,572	443,083	465,293	491,524	533,242	606,921
New Jersey	906,096	1,131,116	1,444,933	1,883,669	2,537,167	3,155,900	4,041,334	4,160,165	4,835,329	6,066,782
New Mexico	91,874	119,565	160,282	195,310	327,301	360,350	423,317	531,818	681,187	951,023
New York	4,382,759	5,082,871	6,003,174	7,268,894	9,113,614	10,385,227	12,588,066	13,479,142	14,830,192	16,782,304
North Carolina	1,071,361	1,399,750	1,617,949	1,893,810	2,206,287	2,559,123	3,170,276	3,571,623	4,061,929	4,556,155
North Dakota	2,405	36,909	190,983	319,146	577,056	646,872	680,845	641,935	619,636	632,446
Ohio	2,665,260	3,198,062	3,672,329	4,157,545	4.767,121	5,759,394	6,646,697	6,907,612	7,946,627	9,706,397
Oklahoma	....	....	258,657	790,391	1,657,155	2,028,283	2,396,040	2,336,434	2,233,351	2,328,284
Oregon	90,923	174,768	317,704	413,536	672,765	783,389	953,786	1,089,684	1,521,341	1,768,687
Pennsylvania	3,521,951	4,282,891	5,258,113	6,302,115	7,665,111	8,720,017	9,631,350	9,900,180	10,498,012	11,319,366
Rhode Island	217,353	276,531	345,506	428,556	542,610	604,397	687,497	713,346	791,896	859,488
South Carolina	705,606	995,577	1,151,149	1,340,316	1,515,400	1,683,724	1,738,765	1,899,804	2,117,027	2,382,594
South Dakota	11,776	98,268	348,600	401,570	583,888	636,547	692,849	642,961	652,740	680,514
Tennessee	1,258,520	1,542,359	1,767,518	2,020,616	2,184,789	2.337,885	2.616,556	2,915,841	3,291,718	3,567,089
Texas	818,579	1,591,749	2,235,527	3,048,710	3,896,542	4,663,228	5,824,715	6,414,824	7,711,194	9,579,677
Utah	86,786	143,963	210,779	276,749	373,351	449,396	507,847	550,310	688,862	890,627
Vermont	330,551	332,286	332,422	343,641	355,956	352,428	359,611	359,231	377,747	389,881
Virginia	1,225,163	1,512,565	1,655,980	1,854,184	2,061,612	2,309,187	2,421,851	2,677,773	3,318,680	3,966,949
Washington	23,955	75,116	357,232	518,103	1,141,990	1,356,621	1,563,396	1,736,191	2,378,963	2,853,214
West Virginia	442,014	618,457	762,794	958,800	1,221,119	1,463,701	1,729,205	1,901,914	2,055,552	1,860,421
Wisconsin	1,054,670	1,315,497	1,693,330	2,069,042	2,333,860	2,632,067	2,939,006	3,137,587	3,434,575	3,951,777
Wyoming	9,118	20,789	62,555	92,531	145,965	194,402	225,565	250,742	290,529	330,066
TOTAL	38,558,371	50,155,783	62,947,714	75,994,575	91,972,266	105,810,620	122,775,046	131,669,275	151,325,798	179,323,175

[1] According to the Bureau of the Census